A Devotional Alphabet

Sixty-second meditations for women
to guide them on their faith journey

Amy Schisler

Bozman, MD 2019

Copyright 2019 Amy Schisler

Chesapeake Sunrise Publishing

ISBN: 978-1-7322242-8-5

Published by:
Chesapeake Sunrise Publishing
Amy Schisler
Bozman, MD
2019

*T*able of Contents

*D*ear Readers,

The devotions contained in this book were previously printed as blog posts (citations are at the bottom of each page). As I travel on my spiritual journey, I am growing in my love for God and my desire to share Him with others. These devotionals are meant to bring you closer to God and help you travel on your own journey from this life to the next.

Since my blog is based on my own life, my family is often a central component. My husband, Ken, is my rock, and my writings reflect that. He is mentioned often as are my children. Rebecca, our oldest, is finishing law school as of this writing and will be married next fall. Our daughter, Katie, is in college, and our youngest, Morgan, just started college. They are my inspirations. I also write a lot about my parents and my father-in law who completed his journey in 2018. My friends, near and far, are also staples, especially George, and the rest of my Holy Land Pilgrim Families.

We are all on a journey. Some will travel longer and farther than others. Some know their desired destination, and others are new to the promise of Heaven. I hope these humble writings help light the way for you.

$\mathcal{A}$ppreciate The Gifts From God

"The secret of happiness is to live moment by moment and to thank God for what He is sending us every day in His goodness."
- St. Gianna Molla

Today, one can watch an Olympic hockey team go from being the underdogs to Gold Medalists and declare it a "miracle" yet be unable to recognize that real, faith-infused miracles actually exist. The cry of a newborn baby, the survivor of an accident in which nobody should have been spared, the chance meeting of two people destined to be together—these are not simply random happenings, cosmic chaos, or unexplained phenomena made right.

What is so wrong with believing, not only that all things are possible with God, but that all things are possible because of Him?

As for me, I subscribe to the belief that every day lived is a miracle and that true miracles exist all around us. Why would anyone want it any other way?

Do You Believe in Miracles? April 26, 2017

Much debate has taken place about Jesus's admonition to "let the dead bury the dead." Some say Jesus was referring to the "spiritually dead." Others say that Jesus was telling us to not look for excuses to avoid following Him. In thinking about those I've lost over the years, I wonder if there is a deeper, hidden meaning.

How often do you attend a funeral at which it seems the entire world comes to say goodbye? How many people reach out, after someone is gone, to say they hadn't seen the person in years and regretted not getting in touch. How many times have you lost someone and cried that you let so many other things come before spending time with that person?

Perhaps Jesus was reminding us that, while taking care of the dead is a good thing, it's too little too late. Maybe we should have been paying attention to that person, to their needs (spiritual and physical), to their joys and sadness, long before they were gone.

Who do you need to reach out to today?

Let the Dead Bury The Dead, July 4, 2018

I wonder if the rich man in Jesus' Parable had more than just possessions. Did he have a family? Did he have friends? Was he in good health? If he were alive today, would he awaken and be grateful for all that he has? Would he look at the riches and blessings that he has and know in his heart that he doesn't need more? Would he recognize that all he needs to make him happy is love? The love of God, the love of others, and love for himself as he is, without possessions, without riches, without STUFF.

We live in a world where the grass is always greener on the other side. We always want what someone else has, and sometimes we want the impossible. We ask for more and more; we work longer and harder so we can buy more. We do this even though our closets are bursting, our drawers won't close, and our cups runneth over. And how happy are we? Even with a family, a home, electricity, hot food, cars, and coffee, are we still looking for more? When will we be satisfied? When will we realize that we have enough? When will we realize that love is all we need? That it is love that makes us wealthy, not things.

The Greatest Christmas Gift You Can Give
November 28, 2018

When we gather around Mom's dining room table at Thanksgiving, we all take turns thanking God for what we are most grateful. That includes the presence of every person at our table and those no longer with us. Then we will feast on turkey and stuffing, sweet and mashed potatoes, Grandma's famous rolls, a plethora of vegetables, and (my own favorite) my father's incomparable fried oysters, fresh from the Bay. One of our traditional favorites at every holiday meal is my Godmother's baked pineapple, a delicious mixture of pineapple and other ingredients that melts in your mouth

At some point over the holiday, we will take part in a rousing run of Dominoes, from the double fifteen down to blanks and a hilarious game of charades. There will be a lot of eating, a lot of driving, and a lot of family togetherness, and I wouldn't have it any other way. It's these times for which I am most grateful.

What is your favorite holiday and for what are you grateful?

Giving Thanks, November 26, 2014

One Father's Day, I surprised Dad with fly-fishing lessons. Dad was so surprised, and we had a great time learning together.

Each morning and evening for the next week, Dad and I stood in silence, casting our lines. What a peaceful and beautiful experience it was. We enjoyed the tranquility as we cast our lines and hoped for a bite. We never did have the trout dinner of which we all dreamed.

We did, however, witness a stunning bobcat as it came out of the woods and slinked down to the river for a cool drink. After a few minutes, it looked up at us with its lazy gaze, then bent back down for another sip before padding off into the trees. Dad and I looked at each other and smiled.

There are few times in life when we have the opportunity to *just be* with someone we love, not talking or watching a movie or being part of the crowd, but just being together, enjoying the moment and each other's company. I've never had a similar experience with anyone else, and I think it's the closest thing to Heaven that I've ever felt.

How often do you let yourself *just be*?

Casting for Memories, August 26, 2015

When I was a little girl, I wanted to be a great many things—librarian, teacher, writer, artist (I don't know what I was thinking—ZERO talent there), and even a nun. In high school, I was focused on law, though Mrs. Wilson always told me that I should be a writer. In college, I went from lawyer to speech writer to history teacher, and then, finally, back to librarian. I always knew I wanted to be a wife and mother. Never did I think about how much money I would make, how big my house would be, or how much wealth I would have. My end goal was always to be happy. So, it's kind of funny now that I look around and see how rich I've become.

God blessed me with wealth beyond my wildest imagination. I may never have diamonds on every finger or a waterfront estate or enough money to feed all the poor in the world. But what I do have is treasure far greater than any ever sought by kings. I thank God for my riches every day.

Do you recognize your wealth and thank God for it?

I Never Imagined I Would Be This Rich
August 23, 2017

Sometimes, I can't help but wonder... as my girls were growing up, as they were experiencing all of the wonderful things we did, visiting foreign places, and learning how to navigate the world, did I remember to teach them the importance of wisdom? What do I mean by that? Intelligence is a function of the brain. Worldliness is a function of experience. Doing well in school comes as a result of hard work and studying. Not a single one of those has anything to do with wisdom. Wisdom is a gift of the spirit and comes entirely from God.

In a reading from the book of Sirach, we hear the importance of wisdom. It is elusive but can be found and should be sought by everyone. Those who know wisdom (personified as a woman in the text) love life, inherit glory (heavenly, not earthly), receive blessings, overcome fear and dread, treasure knowledge, and understand justice. Wisdom comes through hard work, perseverance, and trust in God. You can't learn it from experience or by reading a book. It only comes from spending time with God. It is a gift we should all seek.

Are you seeking wisdom in your life?

How Many Licks Must We Take? February 27, 2019

*B*elieve in Daily Miracles

"We must not become so preoccupied looking for 'major' miracles that we miss all the daily ones." - Mark Hart

I love creating our annual photo album and looking back over the year, thinking about all that we did and saw. There were many life-changing events, but the things that make me smile the most are the things, large and small, that bring to mind the phrase, 'wonder and awe.'

I still remember being in 8th grade, preparing for Confirmation, and learning about the Gift of the Spirits. Sr. Janet told us that the most important gift was wonder and awe, which she described as always seeing life through the eyes of a child, unjaded and full of amazement at all that God does, creates, and gives. Her words have always stuck with me, and I have been reminded of them many times throughout my life.

Do you still use your gift of wonder and awe to see the many miracles in our world?

Through the Eyes of a Child, January 11, 2017

There's something about a sunset, isn't there? It's more than just the beautiful colors across the horizon and the way the sun dips just behind it all until the edge of the Earth seems to drink it in and swallow it down. No matter where I am in the world, I am fascinated by sunsets. Oh yes, a sunrise is beautiful and signals the beginning of a new day, a new chance, but I love a good sunset.

While there are many roads you may travel tomorrow and adventures still ahead, all we have when we are called home is what we did and how we lived today, and yesterday, and the days before. Every sunset allows us to assess our day and our actions, to bathe in the glory of our current existence, and to relish in the simple things in life. To watch a flaming ball of fire as it falls into the ocean where it is extinguished amid a palette of blues, purples, and pinks is a daily miracle not to be taken for granted.

Where will you be at sunset tonight?

The Message of the Sunset, October 29, 2014

When my father was diagnosed with cancer, about ten years ago, he sought all the medical help he could find. He did everything the doctors prescribed. And he prayed. Daily. With the profound belief that God would hear his prayers.

Dad is now eighty-two and as healthy a as horse. A miracle? Perhaps not, but there are proven medical miracles that even doctors can't explain. Many of them.

Studies show that those of us who do believe in miracles experience increased satisfaction in life and greater protection against the negative effects of stress. Perhaps that's just by chance. As for me, I subscribe to the belief that every day lived is a miracle and that true miracles exist all around us. Why would anyone want it any other way?

Do You Believe in Miracles? April 26, 2017

So many people spend their lives searching for more: more wealth, more stuff, more power, more friends, more time. When will people realize that all we need to feel happy is to be content with what we already have? It's not about keeping up with the neighbors. It's about finding joy within yourself and radiating it out to others. It's not what others give to you but what you give to them that will bring true satisfaction with what you have and who you are. It's about recognizing the little miracles we witness every day.

I implore you to look past the stuff and see the simple miracles that surround you at every moment. Laugh at the kids building a snowman in your yard or next door. Delight in the smell of the flowers in your garden in the spring. Close your eyes and revel in the feel of the warm sun on your face. Breathe in the crisp, cool fall air. Don't let a minute go by without noticing all of the amazing things in this world. Find your sense of wonder and awe, and cherish it. Never stop looking at life through the eyes of a child. You will find that miracles abound.

What miracles can you witness today?

Through the Eyes of a Child, January 11, 2017

*C*hannel Courage

"Be strong and courageous. Do not be afraid, do not be discouraged, for the Lord your God will be with your wherever you go." - Joshua 1:9

My daughter, Katie, and I were doing a ropes course together. We were the only females in our group of two dozen or so people to conquer all five courses, part of a small handful of women who attempted the courses that day. After we finished, the men offered us congratulations and compliments, and a woman waiting at the end, high-fived us, telling us that a man called us the Warrior Women.

We all have the ability to be Warrior Women, to encourage one another, see each other for what we give and not what we lack, be there for each other in good times and bad, and inspire others to have faith in themselves, each other, and God. May we all be blessed with a Warrior Woman, or a group of Warrior Women, in our lives.

Are you courageous enough to be a Warrior Woman to others?

Friends and I were talking about how hard it is to raise children in today's world. We worry about our children. Will they make the right decisions, meet the right people, find the right job, make it to school or work and back safely, be safe at school or work, survive to be an adult, a parent, a grandparent? It's a constant state of worry.

Worry like that can be crippling, immobilizing, even life-threatening. So, what's a mother to do?

We all came to the same conclusion. We just have to hope for the best, put our trust in God, and love our children fiercely every day. We can't lock our children in a tower (that never works in Fairy Tales), and we can't live our lives in constant fear, nor do we want to teach our children to live their lives in constant fear. We want them and ourselves actually LIVING! We have no other choice but to teach them right and wrong, instill in them a solid set of values and morals, and pray for them every day. We need to lead with courage and teach them to do the same.

What are you afraid of? Have you prayed about it today?

Be Not Afraid October 7, 2015

Suddenly, the light through the trees became bright as understanding dawned on me. I was in a meeting with a wonderful group of women whom I am so lucky to be able to call my friends. Many of us have been meeting every other Monday for the past fifteen years. We pray, discuss, read, and learn, and some of my greatest revelations have come from those Monday morning meetings.

We were watching a short video in which we heard, over and over, people saying that they worried, were never content, and were constantly searching for happiness and meaning in their lives until they realized they could only find true joy in God. When they learned to let Him guide them, take away their cares, and be the light at the end of their tunnels, their lives changed. That's when it hit me. The key to contentment is knowing that there are many things in this world simply beyond our control. All we can do is have faith that the everything will turn out okay.

Are you facing your fears, knowing that God is on your side?

Saying Goodbye to Worry and Regret
November 9, 2016

I had been going to physical therapy for three weeks after months of waking up with severe upper back pain. I was shocked when I learned that the pain was due to the deterioration of my muscles because of my bad posture.

Who would have thought that poor posture would actually lead to a reduction in the rotation of my shoulder? Alas, that was the diagnosis, and the doctor said it needed to be fixed now before it was too late. However, fixing the problem is, at times, more painful than the aching back muscles. Sometimes, I just want to give up.

And isn't that how we often feel about the things that are hard, things that cause pain, things that make us wish there was a magic spell to make everything okay?

At some point, we all have to change course, break our bad habits, learn to sit a little straighter, walk a little taller, push back our shoulders, and hold our heads high, having courage that God will never lead us astray.

What are you facing today that is causing you pain? Do you have the courage that God will get you through it?

Standing Straight and Reaching New Heights
September 26, 2018

There is a season for all things. We've read the verses or heard the song. Every school choir seems to sing it at some point. It's been in movies and in books. Many reflections have been written about the words attributed to Solomon, but I believe there is a line that is missing, something that each of us experiences again and again throughout our lives—a time for change.

One could argue that every line in the passage is about change, and that is true. Birth and death bring change as do tearing down and building up. Scattering and gathering can be catalysts for change as can seeking, losing, keeping, casting, rending, sewing, speaking, loving, etc. We are faced with changes, both large and small every day.

Change is inevitable. The only thing we can do is embrace it and grow from it. Even changes that are bad or rip us apart, can lead to a new understanding, perhaps a new friend, or new way to look at life. We need to have the courage to accept and embrace change and see each change as a blessing, a chance to learn and grow, and a season to be welcomed.

Do you accept change with courage?

A Season for Changes May18, 2016

I always feel like I'm in the minority, but I love change. I welcome change. I open my arms to it and let it fill me with possibility. Like the arrival of the beloved nanny who appears on the winds of change, we never know what's going to happen when there's a shift in the current dynamic. Rather than cower and despair when change is upon us, I see things the way that Mary Poppins sees them, "We're on the brink of an Adventure. Don't spoil it by asking questions" (P.L. Travers, *Mary Poppins Comes Back*).

Life is about change. Like the weather, it can be unpredictable but inevitable.

Greet change with excitement, and embrace the changes that come your way—a new job, a new school, a new boss, a new home, a new city. Whatever life throws at you, seize the golden moment, the sunrise as well as the sunset—the beginnings and the endings. And when the changes you encounter cause you to retreat and reassess, take that as a sign that it's time to react. As a very wise man once said, "Be the change that you wish to see in the world" (Mahatma Gandhi).

How do you face change?

Embracing Change January 9, 2019

*D*angerous Liaisons: Technology

"We are no longer able to hear God. There are too many frequencies filling our ears."
- Pope Benedict VXI

We were watching a movie in the backyard when Rebecca looked around and said, "Every one of you is playing a game on your phone or iPad instead of watching the movie." I was as guilty as the rest. Watching a movie in the backyard with my family, with a glowing fire blazing nearby, and two dogs slumbering next to my chair, should be all the entertainment I need. Why was I on my phone?

We are on them ALL. THE. TIME. At dinner, the movies, the subway, walking down the street. What is so important that none of us can go more than ten seconds without looking at our phones?

Today, focus on the good in your life, go outside without your device, try something new, see the world, imagine the possibilities, discover the people around you, and be grateful for what you have. No phones necessary.

Seven Reasons to Put Down Your Electronic Devices This Summer June 14, 2017

Open your eyes to the world around you. Don't sit with your eyes glued to a screen. You'll never experience the virtual world like you can with all five of your senses.

Instead of texting friends, go out with them. Turn the phones off and enjoy your time together. When you have a problem, need a shoulder to lean on, or someone to wipe your tears, your phone won't meet your needs. Only your friends, live and in the flesh, can give you a hug, a pat on the back, a genuine smile and loving touch.

Life slips by in the blink of an eye. A sunrise may last for as long as thirty minutes, but each minute is completely different. Colors change, clouds shift, shadows grow and shrink. Each moment, the scene transforms. It's an amazing palette of colors on an ever-changing canvas. To look away for even an instant is to miss the next great work of art.

Perhaps God does that on purpose as a reminder that each moment, each tiny piece of time is to be marveled at, revered, appreciated. Today, put down your phone and seek the real thing.

Six Reasons to Put Down Your Phone!
July 20, 2016

I sometimes wonder if today's young people have any idea that they can actually exist without being on their phones.

It's why I love our second home in Southern Colorado. Out there, it's a time of no texting, no chatting, no posting, and no calling. For the first twenty-four hours, our kids and their friends aren't sure they can survive. Then, slowly, they start to come alive. They notice the low-hanging clouds over the mountains, the way the morning mist clings to the treetops, and the wildlife that lives around the mountain. They go four-wheeling to look for deer, and they begin to talk about which day they are going to get up at five to see the sunrise.

I like to imagine that the kids, once home, might actually think twice the next time they face the choice between their phones and a bike ride, or a walk in the woods, or any other activity. I hope that the one thing they will remember the most about our time away is how wonderful life is when you stop letting other things get in the way of actually enjoying it.

What will you do today that doesn't involve your phone?

Off The Grid August 10, 2016

My husband, Ken, gets very frustrated when we go on long drives and everyone has their eyes glued to some kind of screen.

"Look around you," he'll cry. "You're missing all the good stuff."

As much as I love to read in the car, I know he's right.

When everyone is staring at their screens, they're missing the real show outside their window.

Luckily, my girls have been able to experience some of those beautiful things They've slid down a snowy hill on a warm, sunny day in the middle of July. They've white-water-rafted in the Rocky Mountains. They've kayaked in the Gulf of St. Lawrence. And not once during any of those times did they ask, "Where's my phone."

Find something to do today with your loved ones that takes them outside and away from technology.

Seven Reasons to Put Down Your Electronic Devices This Summer June 14, 2017

We all think we know someone and what's going on in their life, but we don't. Sometimes we see only the good, blind to what's really going on with family and friends. We see their happiest moments, posted on social media, and often forget to ask about the tears they shed for a loved one, the defeat they just suffered at work or on the field, the problems they are facing with their family, or the devastating news they recently received.

Social media lets us forget that we're all real people. We need human interaction, and not the technological kind. We all have basic human needs. We need *REAL* friends.

The next time you're scrolling through those smiling, happy photos plastered on Instagram, remind yourself to stop and think about the faces you're seeing. Ask yourself when the last time was that you contacted them, asked about their families, inquired about a hard situation they were in, or checked on their health.

Don't let today go by without checking on someone—face to face or by spoken word.

Friendly Deception – how social media is changing our relationships and what we can do about it
October 3, 2018

*E*at, **Pray, Love: Family Time**

"The sun looks down on nothing half so good as a household laughing together over a meal."– *C. S. Lewis*

We watched as the shadow of the sun traveled across the blood moon, leaving just a sliver of light on the right side of the moon's face. We stood as long as we could before heading back upstairs to get ready to start our day.

How often do you take a moment to celebrate life with your family? It's not always easy! When my Morgan groaned and complained that she didn't want to get up that early, it would have been easier on her, and honestly on me, to let her sleep. But somehow, I knew that the real joy in standing on the chilly porch in our pajamas wasn't seeing the cosmic phenomenon, it was seeing it together as a family.

Our time here is so fleeting. We are here today and possibly gone tomorrow. Take the time to do those little things that will make your family life memorable. Then nobody will never have to ask you, "Did you miss it?"

Did You Miss It? October 8, 2014

Food isn't just sustenance for our bodies. In some ways, it's nourishment for our souls. It creates a connection, a memory, a return to a cherished place in time long ago. I can't taste hot chocolate without remembering how my mother always, so lovingly, had it ready and waiting for us when we walked into the house on a bitterly cold day. My father remarked recently that bread pudding reminds him of his mother and the wonderful dessert she made, using day-old bread. The smell of Southern Maryland stuffed ham takes me back to holidays with my extended family in St. Mary's County, Maryland.

They say you are what you eat, but I think it's more like, we become who we are partly through the foods we eat and love. They help form attachments, create cherished memories, and serve as a reminder of the people we love and those we've lost.

At your next family meal, every bite you take, and remember with fondness those loved ones whose recipes have been passed down through your family. Let this meal and this time together create memories that will last a lifetime.

Food Memories November 22, 2017

Years ago, my mother wrote an article for a magazine about her grandmother's kitchen table. The sturdy, wooden table, made by my great-grandfather, found a new home when my mother's sister married. Every scratch, every dent, every mark on the table tells a story. My mother remembers it as the place where all news was shared—both good and bad. It was where my great-grandmother sat each morning and said her daily prayers. It was the site of many card games and where weddings, funerals, and family events were planned. It was the one piece of furniture that evoked the true meaning of a home—a place where everyone gathers to share the best and worst in life.

In my house, the kitchen is always the place where we gather. It's where meals are shared, plans are made, discussions are had, birthday candles are blown out, homework is done, and games are played.

My girls laugh at me when I tell them that I plan on having family dinners every Sunday that they are expected to attend, but we all know what my mother's family knew all those years ago—there is nothing that says home, no furniture that says love, like the family table.

The Family Table April 11, 2018

We have a new kitchen table in our home. We had it custom made to match our kitchen and to accommodate our future family (God willing). It seats twelve and two more can be added in a pinch. It's been a host for large school and volunteer projects, crab feasts, craft projects, Christmas cookies, big buffet dinners, holiday gatherings, and more. It's where we talk, laugh, share our day, and plan our night.

Most moms recognize the importance of giving our families a nourishing, filling meal that satisfies our bodies. I believe that the time spent at the kitchen table is also a time to satisfy our souls. Over family meals are most often where stories are shared, dreams are discussed, and plans are prepared.

No matter how many purposes our table has, the most important one is to bring us together as a family. I pray that my kitchen table will always be a welcoming place for loved ones to gather.

How often does your family make a point of gathering at the kitchen table? How about sharing a meal at your table tonight?

We've driven cross-country and back numerous times, to Florida and back a bunch, and to Percé, Quebec down through Niagara. We watched movies, but we also talked, sang, and played games There were fights, and one always poked, pinched, or punched another, but I know our girls would not trade one those family trips.

We always looked at the ride as part of the adventure. We've seen the Corn Palace of South Dakota, the world's tallest sandhill crane, and the largest concrete buffalo. The girls still talk about those things in addition to the many museums and country stores we visited.

What we learned on our trips can be applied to every area of life: you must make an effort to get along with others; you never know what lies around the next bend; there's always more than one route to get to where you're going—choose wisely; don't forget to look around and take a break along the way; keep your sights on your destination, but know that how you get there is just as important.

If you've never taken a family road trip, I highly advise it. You never know what you might learn along the way.

On The Road Again January 7, 2015

Looking back at the simple life my grandparents lived, I wonder where we've gone wrong. Theirs was a life of devotion to their families, their Church, and each other. They took no more than needed and gave more than they had. They bought what was necessary and saved for a rainy day. They paid for everything in cash. They knew that hard work paid off and that God and family were the center of everything.

We're losing our focus on the family. We're losing our respect and love for the elderly. We're losing the grandparent-grandchild connection that made so many of us who we are today. I thank God that my children have grandparents and had great-grandparents to bond with and look up to. I pray that future generations remember how important that connection is.

Grandparents are only in our lives a short time. Cherish them. Build the relationships between your parents and your children. Take the time to see each other in person, spend time together, and show love and respect for each other. Do it today. Someday, perhaps soon, it will be too late.

"Grandchildren are the crown of the aged" (Proverbs 17:6).

Reminders of the Past August 22, 2018

Ken and I realized, almost too late, that our girls were growing up quickly. We recognized as we trudged from one athletic event to another, raced to this awards banquet or that school fundraiser, and squeezed in piano, tennis, and dance lessons, that time was flying by. The precious minutes we had with our children were on the run with "have fun" and "good luck" shouted out the window as we sped off to pick up another child or make it to another event. That's when we decided we needed to set aside one day every month for some meaningful togetherness.

To our pleasant surprise, our girls were all for our new plan to spend time together outside of school or church events or our summer vacation. They liked the idea of doing something fun and out of the ordinary as a family. We went skiing, toured museums, went to the beach, visited Gettysburg, and spent a day at Hershey Park. Where we went and what we did never mattered. Being together was what made it special.

You might be surprised by how much your kids enjoy family time. Plan a day trip with the family and make it a regular event.

Chocolate Memories April 22, 2015

When our children were old enough to play sports for school, the rec sports were wiped off the slate--no travel teams or all-stars, or those other paths to scholarships that most families think are vital to their children's future. Let's face it, only one child on the team is really good enough to get that scholarship. Wouldn't it be better for them to get their homework done and get a good night's sleep instead?

The most valuable piece of advice our high school field hockey coach ever gave us was "Your daughter is very good, but she's not *that* good." Instead of being upset, we were relieved. What a tremendous load off of her back! More time went into academics and less into trying to contact every college coach on the east coast.

We often hear the Pope talk about the importance of the family. How can we improve our family life? How can we find time for family meals? What can we cut out of our children's schedules to make them live fuller, happier, more peaceful lives? How can we reshape our culture to make others see that families matter? What can you do today to instill in your loved ones the importance of family time?

What's Happened to the Family?
September 23, 2015

We no longer live in villages, tribes, or even communal neighborhoods. Extended families live miles, even states or countries apart. Often, both parents work. Who fills the void? Television, movies, peers, and social media. Kids lose their individuality and hide their natural curiosity and intelligence in order to better conform to their peers. They want—no, they *need*—to feel loved and accepted even it comes from a non-loving source. Children who don't have love can experience emotional and physical harm. They fall prey to bullying, shunning, an increase in suicide, and in some cases, teens killing teens. However, there is something we can do to stop this.

We can connect with our families. We can spend time together, eat together, vacation together, talk to each other, *listen* to each other, and help each other. We can ensure that our families are the people to whom our children attach. It's not a matter of politics or continuing a family legacy. It's about helping children to know that they have a purpose in life, that they matter, that they are loved and that they belong.

Tell your children you love them. More importantly, *show* them.

Parent Orientation – Loving our Kids Before it's Too Late September 10, 2016

Times have changed since Laura Ingalls Wilder lived. The West was won, women moved beyond the classroom to the boardroom, and families became too busy to eat together. Mothers no longer cook, clean, and sew all day. Fathers no longer have to hunt for our food. Most children don't walk to school and then return home to work the farm. These are the things that our ancestors worked so hard to move away from, but...

I sometimes long for a few days trapped in the house with my girls, perhaps without electricity, without contact with the outside world, without the demands of our normal, everyday lives. How I miss the days of my own childhood when nothing mattered more than the number of lightning bugs we could catch as we ran through the woods and the farm fields surrounding my grandparents' house. How I cherish the memories of snuggling with my mother while we read together and later, with my own girls. Perhaps, if Laura were here now, she would marvel at how we live today. Or perhaps, she would long to return to the days when her family had little more than love in their *Little House on the Prairie*.

Longing for Laura's Little House February 8, 2017

"Arise, my beloved, my beautiful one, and come! For see, the winter is past, the rains are over and gone. The flowers appear on the earth, the time of pruning the vines has come, and the song of the dove is heard in our land. The fig tree puts forth its figs, and the vines, in bloom, give forth fragrance. Arise, my beloved, my beautiful one, and come!" (Song of Songs 2:10-13).

I start each morning with God. I read the daily Mass readings along with several reflections and meditations, and then I say a daily prayer. Afterward, I usually turn on the morning news and catch the headlines before getting up and heading to the gym.

In those first moments of my day, when the sun is barely over the horizon, my dog always finds her way to Ken's empty pillows (he's a very early riser), stretches herself out the length of the bed, and lays her head on my chest. I am her person, and she reminds me every day how much I mean to her.

I wonder, do I give my human loved ones as much love and attention in the mornings as my dog gives me? Do you?

My Dog Made Me A Better Christian July 17, 2019

*F*orgive Us Our Trespasses as We Forgive Those...

"Forgiveness has risen from the grave!"
- St. John Chrysostom

We could all learn to be better Christians by emulating our canine friends. For example, my dog is always happy to see me even when she should not be.

There are times I'm running late and leave the house without feeding her, yelling upstairs as I hastily depart or sending a family text that she needs to be fed. There are times she wants nothing more than to go on a boat ride with us, recognizing what's going on as we gather the gear, but I tell her no because there are too many people going, or we are docking and eating out. There are times I don't pay as much attention to her as I should, shooing her away because I am too busy or too tired. No matter what I do or don't do, she always comes back, ready to give me another chance. She always forgives, no matter what.

Are you always ready and willing to forgive others?

My Dog Made Me A Better Christian July 17, 2019

Everyone has that friend—the one that nobody can figure out exactly why you are friends. They seemingly have nothing to offer, and perhaps they aren't even that good a friend in their treatment of you or others. There have been times when someone has mentioned one person or another, and I've wondered, "Why do you even put up with them?" But I know what the response would be.

In life, it matters not what someone can do for you. Sometimes, all that matters, is what you can do for them. There are some people in this world who, through no fault of their own, need you more than you need them. Some people have nobody else to talk to, no shoulder to lean on, no one to whom they can vent, nobody to pray for them. Sometimes we need people in our lives to show us that things could be worse or that we shouldn't take anything for granted or from whom we learn to be merciful.

We must remember, "Blessed are the merciful, for they will be shown mercy" (Matthew 5: 7).

Five Things Mother Taught Me May 10, 2017

One of the sites in the Holy Land is Dominus Flevit, where Jesus wept for Jerusalem. On that hillside are thorn trees believed to be the same type of thorns used to crown Jesus. The size and thickness of the thorns is staggering.

The thorns of the Ziziphus Spina-Christi tree will always remind me that few things in life are as small or insignificant as we imagine. Sometimes, what we think of as the smallest sins are actually the large thorns that tear into our souls and separate us from our Creator. I listen to the way we speak to each other with blatant disregard for feelings and feel the punctures to my heart. I recount all the times I haven't been there for others in need and think about those in need of food, shelter, and peace who are receiving little or no comfort, and I feel the piercing of my soul. Can others see the blood as it runs down the faces of those being cut by the thorns we crown them with? Are these the images that Jesus sees when He looks down into the world? Does He still weep?

I pray that we can realize the depth of those cuts. We must all try to avoid the thorns before the damage we do is irreversible, the wounds too deep to heal.

Avoiding the Thorns March 9, 2016

At a Mass in Milwaukee, the priest, Father Timothy Kitzk, told about visiting his family years back when his older sister taught high school calculus. In order to allow his sister to complete her work and spend time with the family, Father Kitzk and his brother offered to help her grade papers. They struggled with marking the answers wrong when the students seemed to have tried really hard but narrowly missed the answer. Father's sister assured them that they had nothing to worry about because she graded on a curve. Father then reminded us that God does the same.

God grades on a curve.

He doesn't look at one act, one sin, one bad decision. He looks at all of our hard work and grades us on a curve. He knows we can't be perfect. More importantly, he knows we can't make the grade on our own. We need His help! We need His mercy. How profound is that?

The homily made me think about how I grade people. I'm certainly not God, but what I say, think, and do matters in the lives of the people I care about. Because the truth is, nobody is perfect. Everybody deserves to be graded on a curve!

Grading on a Curve April 10, 2019

At a penance service, I was reminded of a conversation between Jesus and Peter. Jesus asked the Lord, "Lord, if my brother sins against me, how often must I forgive him? As many as seven times?" Jesus answered, "I say to you, not 7 times but 77 times" (Matthew 18: 20-21).

If Jesus expects us to forgive someone 77 times, how often do you think, in His perfection, God is willing to forgive us? When I look back over my mistakes in life, 77 seems pretty small!

We need to be more like God and let people keep trying, keep forging ahead, keep making mistakes, and love and forgive them anyway. It's not that someone should be allowed to hurt you over and over again but that we should have mercy on others. We need to look past what they've done and see them for who they are. When it comes right down to it, not giving people the benefit of the doubt, not showing mercy, not giving second chances–that might hurt the other person, but it actually ends up taking a toll on you, the person unwilling to forgive or let things go.

Do you need to forgive someone or forgive yourself today?

Grading on a Curve April 10, 2019

Giving of Yourself

"For it is in giving that we receive."
- St Francis of Assisi

I've learned that sometimes it's the unexpected detours in life that force us back onto the right road to our destination. No matter which road we are on, we are all called to love, to serve, and to give.

Whether it's something handmade or homemade, a visit, a hug, or a helping hand, give the gift of yourself to others. It's really the only thing anyone really wants to begin with.

What of yourself can you offer to someone else today?

One Christmas (I was maybe seven or eight) there was a story on the news about a family who had no presents, no clothes, no food, and no heat. The family would be lucky to make it through Christmas. If my parents looked at each other with sadness as we watched the story, I didn't notice. When they discussed it, I don't know. How they found out where this family lived, I have no idea. But one evening, my father came home, loaded us into his car, and drove into the city, to a neighborhood that was rough during the day, not to mention at night. When the door opened, we stood on the step with wrapped gifts, bags of clothes, and food. I'll never forget the tears or the way the woman hugged us. I'll never forget the looks on the faces of the children as they reached for the presents. Maybe some details came from the imagination of a child who witnessed something akin to a miracle, but this is how I remember it.

I don't know what I got for Christmas that year. We didn't have extra money growing up, so it wouldn't surprise me if some, maybe all, of those wrapped presents were meant for us. But I remember there never was and never will be another Christmas quite like that one.

Lighting the Way this Christmas December 14, 2016

I was running errands while Morgan was at field hockey practice. I was standing in the back of the store, weighing my options and trying to decide what would work best, when an older man stopped nearby to look at something.

Before I knew it, this man launched into a story about his younger sister who had eaten a whole box of ExLax as a child. It was more information than I needed to know about this stranger and his family, but I smiled and listened. When he finished his story, I nodded, picked up the plastic containers I'd been eyeing, and began to turn away. But I didn't get far.

The entire time he talked, my mind was screaming, *Don't you get that I have things to do?* But my heart was saying, this man needs to talk.

God knew that this man needed someone to listen to him. He knew that my day would turn out just fine if I spared a few minutes for a stranger. He knew that I'd still be thinking about it today. Maybe that man is still thinking about it, too. And maybe it was just what he needed. You never know when a few minutes of your time will be a true gift to others.

A Little Time to Spare October 11, 2017

When you live simply, you will find that you have more to give. Give your time to help those in need. Give your ear to those desiring someone to listen. Give your words to those seeking comfort and reassurance. Give your talents to the causes that are most worthy. Give money to the poor and your coat to those in need. Share what you have, and never be selfish.

"Then the king will say to those on his right, 'Come, you who are blessed by my Father. Inherit the kingdom prepared for you from the foundation of the world. For I was hungry and you gave me food, I was thirsty and you gave me drink, a stranger and you welcomed me, naked and you clothed me, ill and you cared for me, in prison and you visited me.' Then the righteous will answer him and say, 'Lord, when did we see you hungry and feed you, or thirsty and give you drink? When did we see you a stranger and welcome you, or naked and clothe you? When did we see you ill or in prison, and visit you?' And the king will say to them in reply, 'Amen, I say to you, whatever you did for one of these least brothers of mine, you did for me'" (Matthew 25:34-40).

What time or talent can you give today?

Dear Graduate, Be Happy May 22, 2019

I enjoy the TV show, *God Friended Me*. The main character, Miles, is friended by God on Facebook and tasked with helping people. Miles is convinced that 'God' isn't really GOD, but he has come to believe that his life has meaning, that he is here to serve a higher purpose, that we are all called to help, and that sometimes you just have to stop questioning and start doing.

In one episode, Miles complained that helping people is a burden, and he wished 'God' would leave him alone. Presto! He is unfriended by God, but not before seeing that God sent another friend suggestion. Unable to allow himself to let that person go unaided, Miles spends the show trying to help Rachel, who lost her sister in a car accident. At the end of the show, she tells him that he is the "first person I've ever met...who walks the walk." How awesome would this world be if we all walked the walk!

Have you ever met someone who truly walks the walk? Who lives each day according to the teachings of Jesus, obeying the laws of God over the laws of man? I ask you to join me in trying our best to walk the walk.

Friended By God October 31, 2018

We joined over 30,000 other fans, waiting to get into Shakira's final concert of her tour. It was not my choice for the evening, but it's what Ken wanted. We waited over two hours to get into the Simón Bolívar Parque in Bogota, Colombia. There were no chairs, which did not bode well for someone under 5'5"! Luckily for Ken, he's nearly a foot taller than I am, and luckily for me, there were three giant viewing screens. The concert was great, and Shakira put on a fabulous show. Ken never stopped smiling the entire time.

I was exhausted and didn't know or understand the lyrics. I couldn't see a dang thing other than the backs of the heads in front of me. But Ken sang along with every song, and I got to see him spend an entire evening doing what he wanted to do. Honestly, that's so rare. Ken spends his life making the girls and me happy. He grants every wish and never asks for anything in return. So what if it wasn't the evening I would have chosen? For Ken, it was a dream come true. Though *no me enamoré* (I did not fall in love) with Shakira, I did fall in love a little more with my husband. When was the last time you did something you didn't want to do for someone else?

Me Enamoré November 7, 2018

When Katie was very young, she had some concerning medical issues. Her doctor ordered what I believed to be a series of standard tests. Unalarmed, I told Ken that Katie was to be tested for Cystic Fibrosis. Ken broke into tears, not the reaction I expected. He proceeded to tell me that a childhood friend of his had CF and died at the age of 16. Shocked, and unwilling to consider the possibilities in front of us, I cried and said, "This can't be happening."

Ken insisted on taking Katie to Baltimore. I was a nervous wreck. I spent most of the day in prayer waiting for his call. When he finally called with the news that Katie was okay, he sobbed into the phone, and tears streamed down my face. From that moment on, we've been hard-pressed to say no to any charity that involves helping sick or dying children. We're truly blessed, that Katie grew out of her ailments. It's hard to look at another parent or child facing the unspeakable and not find myself back in those few days of the unknown.

We should all look for ways to give, whether it's money, time, or even a prayer for someone in need. Your true and honest generosity, no matter how small, will be greatly rewarded.

Giving More March 1, 2017

*H*arvesting Friendships

"Friendship is...the instrument by which God reveals to each of us the beauties of others." - C.S. Lewis, The Four Loves

When I was young, I loved sweet and fruity wine. Strawberry and plum were favorites. Today, I prefer Amarone or Chianti, bold, dry reds. As I matured, so did my taste in wine. And in friends.

Most young people want to be part of the "in" crowd. With age, we become more discerning about friendships. Our reasons change for seeking friends. A good friend enhances your life as a good glass of wine enhances your meal.

Make good friends and be a good friend. Be the friend you want to have. Your kindness, compassion, loyalty, and attentiveness will come back to you. It's never too late to start. At Cana, the headwaiter remarked, "Everyone serves good wine first, and then when people have drunk freely, an inferior one; but you have kept the good wine until now." Be the good wine for others. Your life will be sweeter in the long run.

6 Ways Friends are Like Wine February 24, 2016

The play, *Wicked*, is a beautiful celebration of friendship. When parting, Elphaba tells Glinda that people come into our lives for a reason, that we are led to those who help us to grow. They agree that no matter what has happened in the past or what may happen in the future, their friendship has changed them, *For Good*. The song tells us that their stories have been rewritten, because they are friends.

I can honestly say that I am who I am today because of those people I call my friends. They influenced who I was as a child, a teen, and an adult. I've had to choose wisely, sometimes letting go of people because their influence wasn't a catalyst for good in my life. I look around me and see who has changed me for the better both as friends and colleagues.

Jesus told His disciples, "Follow me," and they left the lives they knew and followed Him. They felt an instant connection. If we are among the luckiest, we can find that same connection with others. Like the disciples, our stories are rewritten because someone came into our lives. We should strive for those relationships, in marriage and in friendship, that change our lives "for good."

Rewriting the Story September 28, 2016

I would never have formed the bond that I have with my sisters in faith from across the country if they hadn't been so open and trusting with one another, so supportive, and so faith-filled. There is no judgement there, no attempts to be better than anyone, no pettiness or cutting each other down. There is just pure love and the understanding that each of us is here just trying to do the best we can in a world that is a never-ending challenge. Our friendship is like my day on the challenge course with Katie, in which each thing we did was harder than the thing before, each level rockier, higher, and more challenging. We encouraged each other to push on.

We all have the ability to be Wonder Women, to fight for justice, for truth, for peace, and for love. We all have the ability to encourage one another, to see each other for what we have to give and not for what we lack, to be there for each other in the good times and the bad, to inspire others to have faith in themselves, each other, and God.

Who are the Wonder Women in your lives? Reach out to them today and thank them for being your friends.

Wonder Women August 9, 2017

Not all friends are real friends, and not all friends want you to be the best version of yourself. There are many people in this world who would rather tear people down than build them up.

In a world where it's hard to be yourself, find yourself, and always challenge yourself to be better, it's even harder to find someone else who will stand by your side, loving you for who you are and encouraging you along the way.

The best way to find true friends is to be a true friend. Charlotte, in E.B. White's beloved *Charlotte's Web*, told Wilbur, "You have been my friend. That in itself is a tremendous thing." Do the tremendous thing; be the friend you want others to be to you.

Love may be what makes the world go round, but a true friend is always the one who reminds you, that "You're braver than you believe, and stronger than you seem, and smarter than you think." – Christopher Robin

Does someone you know need a tremendous friend today?

"A Tremendous Thing" June 6, 2018

I entered a lottery on the radio with little hope of being chosen. Those who were picked would go to the Holy Land, and the cost was not insignificant. Knowing it was nearly impossible, I quickly forgot about it. Until the day I got the call.

Now, I think about the way my life was forever changed in the Holy Land. There was the awesome knowledge that I was walking in the footsteps of Jesus. There was the profound experience of sharing this for the first time with a group of people who shared my faith. And there was a mingling of hearts and souls that bound us together in an inexplicable way.

From phone calls and visits to texts and Facebook messages, not a day goes by that I don't communicate, in some way, with multiple people I met on that trip. They are not just friends. They are as much family to me as my own flesh and blood. I cannot imagine life without them. I might never have known before how much I needed these people in my life, but now, I can't ever imagine my life without them

Who are the people you can't imagine life without? Reach out to them today.

I Didn't Know I Needed You…   April 25, 2018

Everything about my most recent trip to the Holy Land was special, meaningful, and life-changing. It wasn't my first visit, but I ended both trips feeling the same way—overwhelmed by all that I saw and learned; sad to have to say goodbye to such wonderful places, experiences, and people; and determined to use the trip as a stepping stone to become a better person.

There's something about spending ten days with a group of absolute strangers, in a mystical land, that automatically causes one to act like a better person, to show the best side of himself or herself. I like to think that it really allows us to show our true selves. Why hide your real self from a group of people you may never see again? Not to mention, in the Holy Land, emotions are always bubbling to the surface, and it's easy to become vulnerable, to open up in a way you've never done before, to shed your mask and let others see the person you are or hope to be.

When standing on the shores of Galilee, one can't help but open heart and mind like the Apostles did when Jesus said, "Follow me." How can you become the person God wants you to be?

A World of Kindness February 2, 2019

*I*mitate Christ

"Christ beside me, Christ before me, Christ behind me, Christ within me, Christ beneath me, Christ above me." - St Patrick

It was a cold, snowy morning, when Ken's mother, his brother and sister, and our families met at the farmhouse for breakfast. Dressed in black, steeling ourselves for a day shrouded in grief, we met for a family breakfast provided by the mother of Morgan's boyfriend.

We feasted on breakfast casserole, fruit salad, coffee cake, and pastries. We drank coffee, tea, apple and orange juice. We sat for a solid hour, relishing not only the food but the love and thoughtfulness that brought it to us and that surrounded us. As we ate, we shared stories and memories about Dad. We laughed until we cried, and then, joining the many people who filled the little country church across the road and the reception afterward, we cried until we laughed.

Taking a meal to someone in need may seem insignificant but can be a blessing beyond words. How are you called to bless someone today?

From Sorrow, Joy January 17, 2018

When my father-in-law was nearing the end, I learned that I am not a caregiver. When I took my turns with Dad, I found myself at a loss for what to say, what to do, and how to comfort him. I tried, but words failed me. Instead, I often found myself not sure how to talk to a man who used to love talking to everyone, telling stories, and hearing tales but could no longer speak or interact. I wanted to help feed him, attend his personal needs, and care for his failing body, but I stumbled on my own insecurities.

And then I watched my sister-in-law so lovingly write to Dad over and over on his white board and coax him to write back. I observed my husband gently guide his father to the bathroom, comb his hair, and change his clothes, all with unwavering devotion and patience. I wiped away a tear as my children gave up time with their friends to tend to their grandfather. I look at these people, and countless others take action when I fear I will do something wrong.; I look at them, and I see Jesus.

Dear Lord, help us to be the face of Jesus for others. Help us to overcome our fears and insecurities so that we may serve you and others. Amen.

Seeing Jesus December 20, 2017

We live in world where God is mocked, where people do as they wish, where pleasure is seen as the only thing worth obtaining, and where we value things, including celebrity and power, over virtues. We live in a world where people claim to be "spiritual but not religious."

We seem to have lost our foundation. So many young people are no longer getting married and are choosing to have one child or none. Many never read or hear or learn about God. And while the vast majority of "spiritual" people believe in God (over 91%), they really have no idea what or who God is, how to relate to Him, or why He is important. We are raising a generation of people who believe that they are their own god, that only their decisions matter, and that being "happy" can only be found through self-gratification. Is it any wonder that evil can so easily slip into and become commonplace in our lives?

What can we do to combat the evil that has taken up residence in our world? The answer is so simple it sounds trite, impossible even. Be kind. Be loving. Be patient. Be compassionate. Be forgiving. BE CHRIST. Be Christ to everyone. Are you being Christ to everyone?

A World Without God October 4, 2017

Ken and I met George on our pilgrimage to the Holy Land. Most of us were there with our spouses, some with friends, a few with their daughters, but George was alone. At least, or so we thought. But as we got to know one another, we realized that George was never alone. In the pocket next to his heart, he carried a photograph of his beloved wife, Josi. The trip was one they had wanted to make together, but while George joined us, Josi lay in the nursing home, suffering from early-onset dementia. When we all renewed our wedding vows at Cana, George stood, holding his photo of Josi, and renewed his vows with us, as faithfully committed as ever to his bride.

We've become very close to George, and by extension, to Josi, who now lives with God. Our girls love George and consider him family. He has brought much joy to our family, but more than that, he has brought hope. He allowed us to share in his love for Josi as well as his unwavering faith. He taught us all so much about love, acceptance, trust, and faith. He taught us how to be Jesus.

Is your life an imitation of Christ's life and sacrifices?

A Love Without End April 5, 2017

As a child, I was closer to my grandparents than anybody else in the world. I spent my summers at their home and learned many lessons about life and love. With the world the way it is today, I think everyone could benefit from their wisdom.

My Grandfather always went with us to Mass though I'm told, that wasn't always the case. He grew to in his faith as we all do. It wasn't unusual to find a nun or a priest at the dinner table, nor was it unusual for one of my grandparents to say "Get in the car, we're dropping off [fill in the blank] at the church." Sometimes it was laundry or dinner, other times it was an apple pie or a pail of fresh-picked cherries. Grandma prayed every morning, and I still marvel at her ability to put everything else aside, every day, to spend time with the Lord. They lived Joshua 24:15, "as for me and my house, we will serve the Lord."

My grandparents taught us many lessons but never spoke them out loud. Everything we learned came from observation. They lived each and every day according to the teaching of St. Paul, "Be imitators of me, as I am of Christ" (1 Corinthians 11:1). I pray that I am worthy of their legacy.

"Be Imitators of Me" June 22, 2016

We should strive to be the embodiment of Christ's light.

Jesus told us, "You are light for the world. A city built on a hill-top cannot be hidden. No one lights a lamp to put it under a tub; they put it on the lampstand where it shines for everyone in the house. In the same way your light must shine in people's sight, so that, seeing your good works, they may give praise to your Father in heaven" (Matthew 5: 14-16).

My mother is certainly the light of Christ for all to see. She is patient, loving, kind, humble, sincere, honest, and trustworthy. She puts everyone else before herself and gives without asking for anything in return. If I can be half the person my mother is, emit just a single beam of the light she radiates, then I will have become the best person I can be.

Is there someone in your life who truly embodies Christ? How can you be more like that person?

I traveled to Austin, Texas, to join 300 other women for a weekend of spirituality and fun. Joining me in Austin were thirteen of the women I met on our pilgrimage to the Holy Land a few years prior. For some of us, this was a second or third reunion. For many, it was the first time we'd seen each other since February of 2016.

There were tears, prayers, and much laughter. Each of these women has struggled with something—past regrets, infertility, divorce, poor health, rocky marriages, job loss, the death of a child, ailing and infirmed parents, or some other type of hardship. Each has her own cross to bear, and bear it she does, with dignity, grace, and beauty that can't be measured by the human eye. They love without judgement, act without selfishness, and rely on faith in the toughest times.

I look at these women and am overwhelmed by them, by all that they've done, by all that they have to give, by their strength and determination, and by their desire to be Christ to others. At one point, one of the women said to me, "When I grow up, I want to be you." Those words will never leave me because I just want to be like all of them.

Wonder Women August 9, 2017

*J*oy as a Net to Catch Souls

"The life of a true Christian should be a perpetual jubilee, a prelude to the festivals of eternity." St. Théophane Vénard

We are all seeking joy. It is the thing which we most desire, whether we know it or not. Often mistaken for other emotions, joy cannot be captured or contained; it cannot be sustained in this life. We reach for it, long for it, pray for it because it is the thing which our souls most desire. St. Peter said it is "inexpressible and glorious...the result of your faith [felt by] the salvation of your souls" (1 Peter 1:8-9).

Rejoice in and proclaim joy when you experience it. When you feel that tug of your heart, that leap of your soul, cherish it. Hold fast to it with the knowledge that it is but a foreshadowing. Pray to feel never-ending joy on the day promised when "everlasting joy will crown their heads. Gladness and joy will overtake them, and sorrow and sighing will flee away" (Isaiah 35:10).

And remember the words of St. Teresa of Calcutta, "Joy is a net of love by which we catch souls."

Seeking Joy September 18, 2019

Saskatoon, Saskatchewan is not quite a tourist mecca. There are few flights in and out, and there aren't museums with ancient artifacts or amusement parks graced with princesses and fireworks or sandy beaches lined with palm trees. In fact, there isn't much in Saskatoon to draw the average tourist, but we chose that city, smack-dab in the middle of Canada, for a reunion. Why? Because that's where the SaskaPriest lives and leads his flock of parishioners at Holy Spirit Catholic Church. Father is a cheerful man with a reddish beard and big smile whose website is filled with homilies and occasional blogs.

It was Father Darryl Millette who was one of the main catalysts that cemented the friendships of a group of pilgrims in the Holy Land. Father is the epitome of joy with an infectious chuckle and twinkling eyes that make you want to smile. If ever anyone followed Pope Francis' command to live life with joy, it is Father Darryl. Just being friends with him brings us joy, and that joy is radiated in our love for each other. Joy abounds because love abounds.

What brings you true joy?

Where Two or Three are Gathered...
August 21, 2019

Visiting Castel Gandolfo was one of the most amazing things I've done on my travels, not just because of the grandeur of the home and the indescribable acres of beautiful gardens, but because of the people I encountered there.

Walking back down the mountain, it occurred to me that all of those people either loved their jobs OR they truly took the Holy Father's orders to heart.

I don't know about you, but that's the world I want to live in. No, not the summer residence of the Popes, but a world in which each person we meet strives to impart some of their inner joy to everyone he meets; a world where, no matter what sadness or loneliness or feelings of despair we may have, we can still find the joy within, a joy worth sharing with everyone around us. That is the joy that accompanied the suffering on the cross– the joy that we are loved, the joy that we are saved, the joy that this life is just a time of passing through until we all reach our perfect summer residence where the sun (SON) always shines beyond the cross, in spite of our trials, into eternity.

Today, radiate joy to those around you.

A Joyous Reminder September 4, 2019

Many families go out to dinner together and enjoy a nice, quiet evening. The children are quiet as the adults converse over cocktails. They enjoy their meal with impeccable manners and come and go quietly and politely. That is not my family.

It isn't that we don't have manners or that we don't know how to act. We behave just fine when necessary. But the truth is that we like being together, we enjoy the times we share a special evening together, and we definitely like to have a good time.

There are some who look down on us when we're enjoying ourselves, but that's okay. As the waitress said, one uproarious night in particular, "We'd much rather see sisters who make each other laugh than ones who fight all the time." Of course, that sent all of us into a fit of laughter knowing that she hadn't been in the camper with us earlier in the day.

The truth is, given the choice between children who mind their manners but don't experience the true joy of being a family or children who stick out their tongue to show their food and laugh so hard they can't take a sip of water, I'll go for the latter any day.

Laughing Through Life August 12, 2015

Saint John Paul the Great said, "God made us for joy." It's so simple yet so hard. Being grateful can remind us to be joyful.

The more we're thankful for, the more joyful we are. We should note the small things during the course of the day and be grateful for them. Witness the thrill of a child with a new puppy. Savor the taste of a hearty meal or a good glass of wine. Feel the warmth of a fire on a chilly night. Experience the calm of a beautiful song, a good book, or a meaningful prayer. Be thankful for time spent with friends, no matter the occasion.

On a mission trip to Guatemala, Ken was humbled by the poverty he witnessed and amazed by the many expressions of happiness. He said the people had so little but radiated great joy. It reminds me of St. Paul's words to the Corinthians that, as Christians, we should be "in pain yet always full of joy; poor and yet making many people rich; having nothing, and yet owning everything" (2 Corinthians 6:10). When we are grateful, we find true joy. And in finding true joy, we not only create better lives for ourselves but for all the world around us.

Finding Joy in the Most Unlikely Places
November 16, 2016

Greet everyone you meet with enthusiastic joy. St. John wrote, "I hope to visit you and talk with you face to face, so that our joy may be complete." (2 John 1:12).

Whether I've been out of the country for weeks or just at the gym for an hour, my dogs never fail to show their excitement when I return. Sometimes, Misty would be so excited to see me, she would leap up and do twirls in the air. I'm not kidding. Her entire seventy-pound body would leave the ground and spin like a top. If she was outside, she would jump up from her favorite outside napping place on the front porch, leap over the steps, and tear across the lawn, Rosie trailing behind, to meet me when I opened my car door.

What a world it would be if we all greeted each other with such unbridled joy!

$\mathcal{K}$indness Matters

"Actions speak louder than words. Let your words teach and your actions speak." - St. Anthony of Padua

Have you ever met someone who exuded kindness? This is a person whose eyes catch you, twinkle, and without words, bid you a good day. The kind of person who holds out his hand to help you down from a bus, or pulls out a chair for you, or offers to carry your suitcase even though he has one of his own. The kind of person who talks little about himself or herself but offers to listen, without judgement, to whatever is on your mind, offering a smile and encouraging word.

I've said before that kindness is all that really matters and meeting a truly kind person can alter your attitude, your day, even your life. How often do you meet such a person? Once a day? Once a month? Once in a lifetime?

And may we strive every day to just be kind. If everyone were to make that one little thing the cornerstone of all we do, imagine what a wonderful world it would be.

A World of Kindness February 20, 2019

My grandfather is what we are missing in this world. We should strive every day to be like him and raise our children to be like him, to respect everyone; treat all as if they matter; love our friends, family, and God with all our hearts, and show that love at all times; open doors and tip hats; work hard; live within our means; go to church and understand that it's the least we can do as children of God; smile at everyone; make each moment count; and always try new things, make new friends, achieve a new goal, or search for a higher purpose.

I often pray that we can all come to recognize what our world has become and vow to stop this plague of unkindness from spreading. Let's all try to live lives of charity, love, respect, honor, and goodness. Let us all, within our own families, plant gardens, harvest fields, build lasting memories, and raise a generation that appreciates what it has, works hard to have a better life, and understands the things that matter. I believe we owe it to ourselves, our children, and our past generations. I also believe that it's never late to try. My grandfather would agree.

Learning from the Past, Changing for the Future
October 19, 2016

St. Paul wrote to the Galatians, "the fruit of the Spirit is love, joy, peace, forbearance, kindness, goodness, faithfulness, gentleness and self-control." It's the guideline for how we should act, speak, live, and treat one another. It's hard, but there's hope St. Paul didn't call these the *Rules of the Spirit*, or the *Commands of the Spirit*. He called them the *Fruit of the Spirit*. These aren't the things that we are ordered to do or the things we are given, but they are what we reap, what we harvest, what we can share with others if we sow them. If we practice the fruit of the Spirit, then we can spread love, joy, peace, forbearance, kindness, goodness, faithfulness, gentleness, and self-control to others, and in return, receive them back.

Starting today, let's think about what we do, what we say, and how we act, especially in front of our children. So often, I find myself reminding my children to be respectful, speak kindly, or act with love. In those moments, I wonder if I have set the example for them, if I have failed as a parent. For if I have not taught my children to be kind, then what does it matter what else I have taught them?

"In the End, Only Kindness Matters"
October 26, 2016

An article was written about a question posed on Tumblr asking for advice: *How can I be kind?* The answer surprised me. In a nutshell, he said to "fake it." Yes, you read that right. The advice was to think about what an actual kind person would do, and just do it. He suggested that over time, even a horrible person could learn to become kind. He proposed that there isn't any difference between doing something nice for someone because you are a saint, and doing something nice for someone because you are evil or selfish and trying to cover it up. It's an act of kindness either way. His advice was to smile, say hello, act interested in what others have to say, and give people the benefit of the doubt.

What if we all did this every day? What if we pretend not to be in a bad mood, not to be angry at someone, not to be disinterested in what someone is saying? What if we actually act like we care about everyone even if we don't? What if it became a habit? Maybe in time, we would learn to be in a good mood, to quickly get over our anger, to actually find an interest in what others are doing or saying, to truly care about others. What if our pretending became who we are in reality?

Be Kind May 27, 2015

When my children would complain about somebody in their class, I reminded them that they have no idea what that person was going through outside of school. Perhaps that person who refused to give up his seat to you on the subway, or the person at the grocery store who grumbled and complained the entire time she was packing your groceries, just received terrible news or is going through some kind of personal turmoil. I think we tend to believe that if somebody looks great on the outside or has a smile on their face all of the time, their life must be perfect. In reality, this is rarely the case. Everybody is going through something all of the time.

The next time you meet up with somebody who isn't in a good mood, smile at them, and be kind. You never know if that small gesture will add the little bit of brightness they need at that moment. Always remember that even those with a smile on their faces and those who always look happy and healthy could have something hidden that is wreaking havoc on their body, mind, or soul. How you treat them and react to them could make a huge impact on their lives and perhaps even your own.

What's Hidden Inside? June 3, 2015

We're raising our children in a world filled with hate. People are not born evil; they become evil, often due to the people and circumstances around them. There is no 'evil gene,' or 'hate gene.' Every person is shaped by events, books, movies, or experiences. What do we teach children when we talk about others, mock them, put them down? What do we teach our children when we turn our backs on the needy? When we act like we're better, know more, deserve more than others? When we hand them everything, make them work for nothing, and don't teach what it is to value someone or something?

Each of us has the ability to rise above our station. We are capable of being good examples, lending a helping hand, biting our tongue, bringing peace and calm to a situation. We are made in the image and likeness of God and can move past our human weaknesses if we're open to the Spirit. We all commit sin and carry a cross but are worthy of forgiveness and the rise to Glory. No matter how badly the world is falling apart around you, smile, be kind, offer words of encouragement and love, and bring light to a world that everyday seems to be more filled with darkness.

An Instrument of Peace March 23, 2016

$\mathcal{L}$et Go and Let God

"Hold your eyes on God and leave the doing to Him. That is all the doing you have to worry about." - St. Jeanne de Chantal

Looking back, every single bad decision I ever made in my life, whether as a child, a teen, or an adult, was made out of fear. What if they don't like me? What if he won't love me? What if I don't do that, say that, try that? The question was always based in fear, and the decision was always disastrous, if not at that time, then later down the road.

On the contrary, every decision I ever made with confidence that it was the right thing to do, was made with complete trust—in friends, my loved ones, my husband, and God. And those decisions have never come back to haunt me.

"Be not afraid," appears more times than any other phrase in the Bible. The message is simple. Whether or not we hear it can make all the difference in our lives.

Are you ready to put your life in God's hands?

Be Not Afraid October 7, 2015

Breathe. We all do it. Ultimately, it's what keeps all of us alive. Without breath, there is no life. About it, songs have been sung, books have been written, and even movies have been made. In the Bible, we are told that God breathed life into Adam. This was the very first breath of life.

I am often asked how I do all that I do. Most people who know me know that I am a rather calm person. It takes a lot to get me befuddled. So, what is my secret? It's simple. I trust in God for He is my strength through which all things are possible.

And I breathe.

Sometimes all I need is a calming breath in and out. Sometimes I need several breaths and a prayer. Other times, I need time and space to reconnect to myself and the world. But at all times, I simply

– need

– to

– breathe.

Just Breathe March 13, 2015

Ken and I were at a crossroads. Ken's job created so much stress for him that he resigned for his health. In a short time, our savings was almost gone. One night, when talking over bullying at the girls' school, my husband had a crazy idea. He, "We've talked about Catholic school; maybe it's time." I thought he'd lost his mind.

We handed the decision to God. If Ken was offered a job with a salary the same or lower than his previous salary, the girls would stay put. If, however, Ken was making anything above that salary, we would take the proverbial leap of faith.

I will never forget the day the call came. It was May, school was almost out, our applications were on hold, and the girls were wondering where they would be that fall. "Call the school," Ken announced with joy. I was stunned "They offered me my dream job. We can stay in Maryland, and I can work at home, and the pay is what I was making plus to the penny, *to the penny*," he emphasized, "exactly what we need to pay the tuition."

God had answered our prayers in the most direct way, but only because we let Him. Do you trust God?

Be Not Afraid October 7, 2015

Life is a great tapestry. We can only see the threads. They don't always make sense. Sometimes they knot. Sometimes they break. At times, the colors run together, or the picture blurs, but the threads are all woven with other threads to create a masterpiece. We don't always know why things happen, what is around the corner, or how our lives will impact and be impacted by others. We do know that we must do our best, work hard, and try to reach the light at the end of the tunnel.

The train will derail. There will be obstacles in the path and delays leaving the station. But God is the conductor. He has promised his people, "in paths that they have not known I will guide them. I will turn the darkness before them into light, the rough places into level ground. These are the things I do, and I do not forsake them" (Isaiah 42:16).

We are faced with detours and roadblocks every day. It's how we handle them that counts. Remember to put your trust in God, hand Him our burdens, and follow His path. Accept that we're not perfect; our efforts may fall short or on deaf ears. We're all working on a masterpiece despite the broken threads and blurred colors.

Let Go and Let God August 28, 2019

A favorite song of mine is the hymn, *On Eagles Wings.* It reminds us that no matter what we are going through, God is there for us. Life can be hard. We never know what curve ball will be thrown our way.

Years ago, a friend of mine lost her long struggle with cancer. She was 45, unmarried, and without children. She had so much life still to live! Shortly after, our world was rocked with the news that a family friend took his life. This young man was just twenty-one years old; his life was only just beginning. My friend died knowing that she was being held, as the song and Psalm say, "in the palm of His hand." The young man, it seems, did not, and I wonder if the knowledge would have made a difference

Every moment of our lives, we held in the palm of God's hand. Whether we feel peace or loss, profound joy or the deepest grief, God is there. Even in the times when we do not feel His presence, He is there. As the Footprints poem says, it is at the times when we need Him the most, that God carries us. I know that I have relied on this belief many times in my life, and my wish for you is that you know that you are always "in the palm of His hand."

The Palm of His Hand March 25, 2015

"We are unprofitable servants; we have done that which we ought to do." Our priest told us that we are called to service here on Earth. We are not meant to spend our lives being waited while others work. We're meant to pitch in, do our share, and contribute to society when and how we're needed. Everything I have ever believed about serving others was summed up so loudly and clearly, I wanted to turn to everyone around me and shout, "See, I'm only doing what I was meant to be doing."

This is the one thing that some don't understand. Yes, committing to several large endeavors while maintaining a home and career is daunting, but it's not tiring. I am busy, but I am not overwhelmed. I keep my eye on the finish line, jumping over hurdles, sometimes sloshing through puddles, but holding a steady pace. Most of all, I don't worry or stress or let fears or uncertainties overcome me. I know I am not doing all the things I take on for myself. I am doing them for the greater good, and that's what matters because I know that God will not let me fail or falter. He will hold me up, guide me, and lead me to success—His success. For I am His servant.

Nine Reasons Why Saying Yes is Not a Weakness
October 5, 2017

Make a difference in the World

"If you can't feed a hundred people, then feed just one." - St. Teresa of Calcutta

Have you ever thought about the difference just one person can make in this world? Saint Teresa of Calcutta said, "I alone cannot change the world, but I can cast a stone across the waters to create many ripples." Throughout time, there have been those who have stepped forward, some in large and others in very small ways, to make a difference.

How are you making a difference in the world? It doesn't have to be a grandiose gesture; it can be just a stone cast across the waters that causes a ripple. Each of us has the ability to influence countless people every day. What is the mark you are leaving on those around you? In some way, it just may be the mark you leave on the world. Make it count.

The book, *The Five People You Meet in Heaven*, takes a centuries old teaching and brings it to life—every little thing you do, every choice you make, affects another person. I have been a mother for almost two dozen years, a Girl Scout Leader for almost as many, a camp director for more than a dozen, and a novelist for the past several years.

I like to think that I have been able to touch the lives of hundreds of people in some way through one of these channels. Every summer, I see the affect that my wonderful camp staff has on the over one-hundred girls with whom we work. I have watched my own mother touch the lives of people she probably doesn't even realize she has influenced. Believe me, there are many, perhaps thousands, who are the people they are today because you came into their lives in some way.

Sometimes, just a smile is enough to change one's outlook or reroute the course of their day. What can you do today to make a difference in someone's life?

Make a Difference in the World June 28, 2017

What would it be like if more people served others instead of wanting more for themselves? Many school systems require students to obtain service hours before graduation, but the requirements vary. Do they learn to put others first and tend to the needs of those who can't take care of themselves? How many Americans have ever done true acts of service? How many worked at a soup kitchen, volunteered at a homeless shelter, or visited the sick or elderly? I confess, I have not.

Does anyone remember President Kennedy's quote, "Ask not what your country can do for you, but what you can do for your country"? He was speaking about service. President Reagan said, "We can't help everyone, but everyone can help someone." If we all gave a few days a year to be of service to others, our world would be a much different and enormously better place. We would all see the world through the eyes of someone else, and more importantly, learn how it feels to do something phenomenal for one another, even if it's as simple as sitting in a hospital and holding the hand of somebody with nobody else to be there for them. So, I ask, how are you being called to serve?

Choosing to Serve April 6, 2016

According to Webster's, to encourage or give encouragement is "to inspire with courage, spirit, or confidence." It's more than giving a pat on the back or simply saying good job. It's the act of inspiring someone, uplifting their spirit, boosting their confidence. Those are pretty lofty aspirations, if you ask me. Think about it— giving encouragement to someone could actually make a difference in a person's life. You could be the catalyst that allows someone to feel victory instead of defeat, experience success instead of failure, or become the person they were meant to be.

The key word in the definition of encouragement is *spirit*. When someone has lost their spirit, they have lost a bit of themselves, perhaps forever. The death of one's spirit can be the death of any positive outlook they may have for the rest of their lives. To encourage one's spirit, to make them feel good about themselves, to boost their confidence, to help them to see the good within, can be life changing.

We need to be persons of encouragement. You will not only change the lives of those you encourage, but you will become a changed person yourself.

Be A Person of Encouragement April 20, 2016

Like trees in a forest, some of us are tall and sturdy. Some are thin and weak. Some need more nutrients than others. Some are always green and vibrant while others need to go dormant for periods of time. Some have long branches to reach out to everyone, some have deep roots to give stability, and some have leaves that quake like the Colorado aspen, shining and waving, welcoming others into the fold.

We should all reach out to others, provide stability, and welcome others in. We should all see each other as trees, accepting those who seem less than worthy, providing strength to those who are struggling saplings, and nourishing others with whatever they need—food, shelter, friendship, or a kind word or deed.

Let's begin looking at each other differently. We can learn a lot from the ecosystem that created and sustains the world's woodlands and forests. I once read that, trees live longer and reproduce more often in a healthy stable forest. Rather than judge, condemn, or criticize, we need to acknowledge and accept the gifts that each person has to offer. All we need to do is begin seeing each other as trees.

Seeing Through the Forest to the Trees
July 28, 2018

My children had a favorite middle school teacher. They loved the respect she showed them, how hard they were willing to work for her, how much they learned spiritually and academically. They recall that even when she was angry, she spoke softly, with a smile. That's what impressed them the most. She never lost her temper, never spoke harshly, never treated anyone with disrespect, and always smiled. I pray they take her behavior and attitude to heart.

Each of us is called to be a better person, the person whom God created us to be. I have a long way to go, but it helps to have examples that we can look to—saints and middle school teachers alike.

We care called be kind, to see every person as deserving of love, respect, and dignity. Every act, every day should be an act of love.

St. Teresa of Calcutta said, "I am a little pencil in the hand of a writing God who is sending a love letter to the world."

May you add your own paragraph to that love letter in all that you do and concerning every person you meet.

Speak Softly, and Write a Love Letter to the World
August 7, 2016

*N*avigating Through Life

"If a man wishes to be sure of the road he treads on, he must close his eyes and walk in the dark." - St. John of the Cross

Life is all about balance. Have you ever given that any thought? We have two eyes, ears, arms, legs, lungs, kidneys, even nostrils. Our bodies are perfectly proportioned (given a genetic twist here and there); and even inside where we might have one organ, there is another organ opposite it that maintains that balance. When you really think about, it's amazing! So how does that matter for the rest of our being? Writer and theologian, Thomas Merton, taught that "Happiness is not a matter of intensity but of balance, order, rhythm and harmony." Sometimes we are in perfect balance within ourselves and our lives, and, well, sometimes we are not!

Maybe today needs to be about tying up loose ends and restoring balance, order, rhythm, and harmony to your life.

Keeping Balance October 22, 2014

In cardio class, we begin with music with a slow beat. During class, the music gets faster as the beat increases. Breathing is strained, hearts race, and movements are more rapid. We get a short break here and there for a drink or a breath, then resume at a faster pace. All thoughts and efforts are focused on precision, proper breathing, and keeping the pace, until we welcome the cool down with small movements and calming breaths.

What a perfect metaphor for life. We start out slow, unsteady, unsure of what lies ahead, focused on learning our steps and finding the beat. We spend our lives running the race, breathing hard, making larger, faster movements in the world. Then, in the blink of an eye, we're forced to find a slower rhythm and breathe easier, knowing we made it through and are stronger, smarter, and more self-aware.

I see wonderful opportunities ahead as I readjust my steps and take deeper breaths. Life is a gift, and it saddens me that it goes by so quickly while we move to an accelerated beat.

Take a deep breath, slow down, keep your rhythm. It's okay to stop and take a breath.

The Rhythm of Life May 2, 2018

George, came to visit and brought Helen, his almost-ninety-four-year-old mother, with him, the spryest ninety-four-year-old I've ever met. Despite the walker, she is eager to explore, meet new people, and experience new things. My girls adore her and couldn't wait to have her visit us.

Everywhere we went, the girls had to be Helen—the car, the restaurants, the dinner table, everywhere. They wanted to hear how she met her husband and about her sons when they were young. They wanted to hear about crocheting, jewelry-making, and other crafts.

That day was so special, so beautiful. Girls who normally spent their spare time running the tennis court or watching Netflix spent the better part of the weekend gleaning morsels of knowledge from a woman nearly eight decades older than them. I'm sure the casual observer would have seen just a group of women sitting at a table; but what we saw was an elderly woman, her eyes sparkling with delight, hanging out with the girls, reliving her teenage years, and remembering what it's like to be young, accepted by the other girls as a true friend. And it was a beautiful sight to behold.

Just One of the Girls July 25, 2018

We all left the family funeral with a great new perspective on life. The homily really struck a chord with all of us.

Father Early likened life to a class in school. He said that, ideally, when we go to class, we work to achieve As; however, Father told us that we should work hard to achieve all Fs in the class of life.

What? All Fs? But why?

Because...

The real gifts in life all begin with the letter, F. In all that we do, we should strive to achieve those Fs. Below are the few that Father pointed out as well as one that I have taken the liberty of adding:

Family, Friends, Faith, Fulfillment, and Fun.

I urge you, go out and earn those Fs. If you do, you will leave this world as an A+ student of life.

In Italy, I visited a vineyard and learned about wine production. Of the steps taken to produce the best wine in Italy, the most telling is the first one. To ensure the award-winning wine is absolutely perfect, the vintner hand picks the most perfect fruit from the vine. The rest is used in what he termed, 'everyday wine.' What love and care goes into the picking! He spends the hottest days of the year, in the blazing sun, painstakingly choosing the very best grapes—not too heavy with juice, perfectly colored, and without blemish.

Have I ever done anything in life with that much love and care? There are things that took hours, months to complete, but they can't compare to standing in the hot sun all day and into the night, picking hundreds of perfect grapes. Why go to such lengths?

Because the vintner saw the production of the best wine as so important, so magnificent, that he could use only the most perfect grapes. He took care and pride in his work, his vineyard, and his wine. Enthusiasm radiated from him. Any task done with that much love, care, and attention could be nothing short of prize-winning perfection. Certainly, there's a lesson there.

Fine Wine   June 24, 2015

When I was growing up, it was well known that my grandmother was a weather-watcher. No matter the day of the week or time of day, she always knew what the weather was going to be, and she was always right. While we teased Gram, we understood that weather was extremely important. There were always weather-based questions to be answered. Was it going to be calm on the water that morning while granddad was out crabbing? Was hail going to fall on his crops? Could Gram hang her wash on the line? What would the temperature be when the fresh vegetables were gathered and the livestock tended? Their lives literally revolved around the weather, and both of my grandparents were quite adept at reading the signs and knowing what the day would be like.

My grandparents were weather watchers, but they were mindful of the amount of time they had. No matter the weather, life goes on. Don't let a few clouds ruin your parade. Dance in the rain, bask in the sun, enjoy the breeze, watch the lightening, feel the snow on your face. Accept each day, despite the weather, with the knowledge that it is a gift. And even on cloudy days, let your sun shine for all to see.

A Little Rain Must Fall May 31, 2017

Life is full of temporary people. One day, I realized: the most temporary person in the Bible was one of the most important.

"As they led him away they took hold of a certain Simon, a Cyrenian, who was coming in from the country; and after laying the cross on him, they made him carry it behind Jesus." (Luke 23:26).

When Jesus' burden of carrying his cross was growing heavier, Simon was there. Simon had no intention of helping Jesus, and Jesus did not expect help from Simon. Simon was there for a few minutes but helped Jesus during His most vulnerable time. Simon literally carried Jesus' burden.

We're all destined to have a Simon, someone who walks into our lives at an unexpected time and helps with burdens we cannot bear on our own. God puts temporary people in our lives on purpose. We don't understand why and won't know a person is temporary until they are gone.

We aren't meant to carry burdens alone. At times, it takes a new person to walk in and help us through. When they're gone, only then do we see how strong, how brave we've really become.

With Every Goodbye, You Learn June 27, 2016
Rebecca Schisler

Many of us have succumbed to the fitness-tracking craze. My father track of the miles he racks up during the day as he walks in the neighborhood and around the house. I monitor my steps to make sure I'm not sitting too long. Some people track every calorie and every "ring" they close on their exercise app.

Think for a moment about what you're tracking and why. Are they the things that really matter and will make a difference in the end? Shouldn't we be tracking...

* how much we give to the poor;
* time spent in Church, in prayer, with God;
* time we spend with our families, children, spouses, parents;
* time we spend listening when others are talking–really, truly listening;
* times we say thank you to our families, friends, cashiers, God;
* those moments in life when we're called to slow down, take a breath, and just be?
* are we remembering to say happy birthday, happy anniversary, I'm sorry, I'm thinking of you, I'm praying for you, or have a nice day?

Are you tracking the things that matter?

Keeping Track January 30, 2019

A wise man told me something I've never forgotten. The first weekend I was home after college, my family attended Mass. Our pastor, Father Paul (now Monsignor Dudziak), asked me how it felt to be a college graduate. I said it felt good but not great because I'd graduated magna cum laude, not summa cum laude, missing the higher honor by less than a tenth of a point. Father Paul nodded without comment and asked me to follow him to the altar. He pointed to the floor and asked, "Do you see this carpet? It was handmade by Persian monks. It took years, because it was intricately planned and woven by hand. They're experts at making rugs and create the finest works of art. But, in every rug they make, they always weave into it a mistake." He looked at me and asked, "Do you know why?" I shook my head, and he replied, "Only God is perfect." Humbled, I blushed and nodded.

Humans are not perfect, and we never will be. Michelangelo said, "The true work of art is but a shadow of the divine perfection." While we all should aim for perfection, we fail over and over again. That is how we learn and grow and become the person we are meant to be.

Nobody's Perfect April 8, 2015

For Christmas, I gave Ken ballroom dancing lessons. I thought it would be easy. After all, I love to dance and took lessons as a little girl. Ken and I used to go dancing all the time before kids. This was going to be a piece of cake. I was so wrong.

We dance every Thursday night for two hours, learning the Rumba, the Waltz, the Salsa, and others. I had to throw everything I knew about dance out the window and begin at step one, literally. It's exhausting and frustrating. I can hear the beat, but Ken cannot. He can grasp the side breaks, but I struggle. We're learning to dance, but we're learning a more important lesson. We're being reminded of the words that were read at our very own wedding over twenty-four years ago:

Love is patient; love is kind; love is not envious or boastful or arrogant or rude. It does not insist on its own way; it is not irritable or resentful; it does not rejoice in wrongdoing but rejoices in the truth. It bears all things, believes all things, hopes all things, endures all things. (1 Corinthians 13: 4-7)

Perhaps those were lessons God intended for us to learn all along.

Dancing Through Life January 31, 2018

Our long weekend in Guadalupe, to me, was a representation of life in general. We all journeyed a long way, some getting caught in flight delays. Some came with extra luggage for what they'd accumulate on the way. Some were unprepared for the great temperature variations throughout the day and ran out of clothes. Some traveled alone, and a few were strangers, invited by friends to come along.

How indicative of our spiritual lives here on earth! Life is short, but we travel a long way in our quest to reach salvation. We meet roadblocks, delays, and detours. We aren't always as good and faithful as we should be, but we carry on, hoping to find the right path. We prepare for whatever life brings us, carrying extra baggage, often feeling the need to unload some of it along the way. Often, we are unprepared and have to make do with what we have. Sometimes, we travel alone, realizing we can rely on the love and care of those sent by God to walk the journey with us. Often, there are strangers amidst our fellow travelers, seeking friendship and a spiritual connection. In the end, we are all on a pilgrimage, searching for something to make our lives more meaningful.

A Journey of Faith August 15, 2018

Remember the wise old owl who was asked, "How many licks does it take to get to the center of a tootsie pop?" When he couldn't figure out the answer, he cheated and bit into the lollipop. I think that's how we approach wisdom. We think we have all the answers, and when unable to solve a problem, we take a shortcut, give up, or give in. The choices can be destructive, and the path covered with thorns. Sometimes, we find ourselves on rocky ground. We think we are being wise and don't understand when things don't turn out the way we wanted. But true wisdom lies with God.

How many licks must we take, how many dead-ends must we find, how many mistakes must we make before we see we're doing it all wrong? We're lacking true wisdom.

All good things come to those who possess wisdom. It's not lack of suffering. It's to "amass riches beyond measure and be honored for their knowledge" (2 Chronicles 1: 11). Solomon, known as the wisest person to ever live, when offered anything in the world, asked God for just one thing—wisdom. Perhaps we would all do well to ask for and seek the same.

How Many Licks Must We Take? February 27, 2019

"*O*ur Gain is Eternal"

"Suffering is a great favor. Remember that everything soon comes to an end . . . and take courage. Think of how our gain is eternal." - St. Teresa of Avila

It was snowing outside, and the temperature was 26 degrees and dropping, yet, as I passed by the dining room, I was reminded that the world won't remain dreary and cold. Outside, snow was on the ground, but inside, flowers were blooming on my table. Though we were entrenched in the shadows of winter, in time, spring would return.

So it is with life. We have cold and dreary seasons, then warm and sunny seasons. Without the cold or snow or rain, we would have no new life, nothing to look forward to, no buds blooming or fruit trees blossoming. Without sorrow, we can't know joy. Without pain here on earth, we cannot begin to fathom the true joy of Heaven that is to come.

Our family was entrenched in the shadows of woe after the passing of my father-in-law, but I knew there would be a spring. Even in the darkest times, there is light.

From Sorrow, Joy January 17, 2018

Losing people is hard, but knowing that the loss was for a reason helps me keep my faith alive. I wouldn't be the person I am today without the temporary people who shaped me in ways I cannot describe. I don't think I would be as strong as I am today if those people had stuck around.

I'd give anything to go back in time and see those people again, or tell them that I love them when I still had the chance. But life doesn't work that way, and I know now that in this moment, I need to treat every person I come into contact with as if it's the last time I'll see them. I need to thank them for helping me in my most vulnerable time, for carrying my burden when I needed it most.

Say "I love you" before you hang up the phone, make plans with your friends every chance you get, tell your professors how instrumental they've been, and smile at a stranger.

Each of these precious moments won't last forever, but they will shape you.

"And you learn, and you learn, with every goodbye, you learn." – *After a While*, Veronica A. Shoffstall

"With Every Goodbye, You Learn" June 27, 2016
Rebecca Schisler

One morning, while Ken and Morgan slept soundly, and Mother Nature covered the trees and fields with a blanket of white, I quietly walked outside in the dark to take photos of the gently falling snow. The world around me was cold, barren, frozen and unwelcoming, but it was absolutely exquisite. My favorite kind of snow softly fell, landing on every branch, leaf, and needle, turning each and every tree into a glowing, white piece of art, a fine sculpture created by the loving hand of God. I was reminded that, even in the coldest times of life, we are still being touched by God.

The next time you experience a time of cold, harsh, and unwelcomed sadness in your life, be it physical, emotional, or spiritual, remember that there is a reason for our suffering. There are things that can be learned, not by the mind but by the soul. Let others see that sorrow and pain do not always have to end in total despair; there is a light at the end of the tunnel. Be strong, courageous, and faithful, knowing that your spring will come, and eternal happiness will be your reward. Remember that there is always the breaking of dawn, even after the coldest, snowiest night.

There's Gotta Be A Little Snow Sometime
January 23, 2019

Our priest pointed out that Jesus never once used the word 'dead' when referring to Lazarus. He said Lazarus was asleep and called him to awaken. Father said we should take Jesus' words to heart. When we go to sleep, we enter another realm of consciousness. We awake refreshed, renewed, reinvigorated, ready to live life to its fullest. It's the same with death. We sleep, only to awaken to new life, renewed, refreshed, reinvigorated to live in the fulness of Christ.

How fitting that this was the Gospel on Josi's last day on earth. For years, she slept, being renewed, refreshed, and prepared to live eternity with the Lord. She was a gift to us, a witness to the will of God rather than the will of society. George's love for Josi, was perfect. His faith and trust in God, sent a powerful message to all. He never lost faith that God was with him every step, no matter how hard or desperate. He knew the road would be hard, heartbreaking even, that many days would be dark and rough. But he held Josi's hand and walked her journey with her, always seeing the light and glory at the end, always trusting that his love for her, and God's love for them both, would never fail.

A Love Without End April 5, 2017

It's easy to forget, when all is well, that life has its share of sorrows. When I'm at my happiest, others are suffering. When others are joyful, I may be grieving. Life is full of ups and downs. We all experience happiness and sadness. We experience comfort as well as pain. Though we may be filled and satisfied today, we may feel empty and disconsolate tomorrow.

I'd been thinking about the highs and lows of life when a reading from Luke 6: 20-26 really hit home. Most people are familiar with the Sermon on the Mount in Matthew, but not everyone knows the Sermon on the Plain in Luke. The two are the same but Luke adds more of Jesus' teachings to his telling. In Luke, Jesus continues his sermon by saying, *"But woe to you who are rich, for you have received your consolation. But woe to you who are filled now, for you will be hungry. Woe to you who laugh now, for you will grieve and weep."*

I needed to be reminded that sometimes laughter can be turned into sorrow and that pain can lead to joy, tragedy can lead to good, a brick wall can lead to a new start on a new road.

Is God trying to remind you of the same?

Turning the Night into Day September 12, 2018

I had spent an hour in Adoration praying for wisdom and guidance. I was searching for answers and divine intercession with a personal matter that haunted me. It stole my sleep and plagued every waking hour. I wanted it to leave me alone, but there were reminders everywhere—the books I read, the shows I watched, and the news I heard every morning. I wanted to escape it but couldn't. It made me angry. It filled me with overwhelming sadness. It made me want to question why, what good could possibly come of it? For an hour, I prayed for an end to the repercussions of this one event and comfort for those affected by it. I prayed for wisdom for the searching and healing for the suffering. I searched for the right words to say, the right things to do, and the strength and wisdom to follow through, to see the search to the end.

I am no different from you. My struggles are my own. My fears are my own. My search will be part of my journey. But aren't you searching for something, too? Aren't we all? How will you proceed? What path will you choose? And when we will attain the gift of wisdom, the realization that the answer is most likely right in front of us, waiting for us to stumble upon it.

Searching for Answers April 3, 2019

Without sadness, we couldn't fully understand joy. Without mourning, why would we find the need to rejoice?

We must embrace the dark times and allow them to shape us into better persons. There is a term that I think of more and more as I get older. It is *redemptive suffering*. It is the Christian belief that all suffering we do on earth is meant to lead us to a deeper relationship with Christ. In our suffering, we experience a small taste of what Jesus experienced in His passion and death. The suffering gives us the opportunity to share in Christ's humanity and to understand one of the characteristics that makes us truly human. It binds us to each other and to Christ. The more we accept our suffering, the more we become like Christ, and the more we are redeemed. It saddens me to hear people say that if there were a God, He wouldn't allow suffering. There is much to be learned from suffering, and not just for the person in pain. It is meant to lead us to a more beautiful place, a place where it never rains, never snows, never pains or saddens. It is meant to lead us to God.

Is your suffering leading you to God?

There's Gotta Be A Little Snow Sometime
January 23, 2019

At our parish church, we have beautiful stained-glass windows that, when the sun shines through, light up the scenes. They are awe-inspiring. But one night, I noticed, in the absence of light, they are no more than dark, meaningless, colorless shapes. They portray only interwoven figures with no faces, no detailed landscapes, no recognizable places or people.

Is that what I look like when I'm not letting God's light shine through? Am I nothing more than a dark, meaningless, colorless shape?

It goes even deeper than physical appearance. Jesus told us, "You are the light of the world. A city set on a mountain cannot be hidden. Nor do they light a lamp and then put it under a bushel basket; it is set on a lampstand, where it gives light to all in the house" (Matthew 5:14-15). We aren't meant to block the light, to walk around in the throes of gloom and despair. We are meant to live a joy-filled life even in the dark times when we don't feel like smiling or serving.

There's always a dawn. Even in our darkest times, we must reach down deep inside and lift off the bushel basket.

Let Your Light Shine Through March 21, 2018

She suffered for over a year after a tragic event altered everything in her life. Forced to move, say goodbye to friends, change career goals, and learn to love herself again, she kept her chin up, made the best of each situation, and remained focused on dealing with what happened, overcoming the hurt and loss, and starting new. It was scary and painful—the largest cross she may ever carry, but she carried it. One beautiful morning, she texted, "It's been one year today. Look how far I've come."

She's happy. She's flourishing. She's shining with radiance and grace. Her brokenness, wounds, and suffering were transformed and renewed. She was resurrected. There are still dark moments, but she has the support of loved ones and professional help. She prays, goes to Mass, and seeks guidance from above. She won't give up, give in, or allow herself to be defeated. It's not easy. Some days she wasn't sure she would make it, but she is stronger, more confident, and more discerning. Her struggles took her to the next level.

I don't wish pain or suffering or grief on anyone. What I wish for everyone when pain comes along, is a road to salvation.

The Path of Thorns and Rocks September 11, 2019

*P*rofessing love 'til death do us part

"It takes three to make love, not two: you, your spouse, and God." - Blessed Fulton Sheen

Why have women all over the world fallen in love with the fictional character James Alexander Malcolm Mackenzie Fraser? I think, because of the way he loves his wife, Clare, the *Outlander*. He moves Heaven and Earth for her, leads armies to find her, risks his life to protect her, and risks his future to save her. He tells her he loves her and *shows* her, and he never fails to remind her that she is his world.

Any author or television producer can create the perfect man, but so can God. Jamie has his flaws. We all do. My husband isn't perfect, but he's perfect for me. I only needed Jamie to remind me that you can tell a lot by the way a man treats and looks at his woman. Those piercing blue eyes say it all. Lucky me, I get to look into my own set of beautiful, piercing blue eyes every day to see unconditional and boundless love. And I don't even need the Scottish accent to hear what they're saying.

Falling in Love With Another Man Made Me Love My Husband More August 30, 2017

When our youngest daughter was born, the first thing Ken said was "she looks just like my sister." The second was, "Oh no, we have to pay for three weddings." Sure, we'll need to pay for their weddings, but I'm not concerned. My concern is not the wedding but the marriage.

Tend to your marriage like it's a garden. Weed out fear, mistrust, judgement, and defensiveness. Prune any hurt that grows there (because it will), and water the seeds you plant—hopes, dreams, and children. Let the sun shine on it every day by complimenting, helping, and most important, talking; and don't be afraid of the rain and storms. Welcome them as ways to strengthen your marriage. Clean up fallen branches after the storm clears, or they will clutter your lives. Because there will be storms, and there will be things to clear away, but by working together, you can weather anything life hurls at you.

Trust that God has brought you together and will guide you. Go to Church together, pray together. Make faith the foundation upon which you build all thing. Remember - with God, all things are possible.

Letter to My Daughters' Future Husbands
July 15, 2015

Did I really know what was involved when I took my wedding vows? Was I simply planning for that one day or truly thinking about my future? Perhaps it has been the same through all generations, but today it seems that marriages are disposable, vows are merely wishes, commitments are fleeting. When marriage begins to falter, we must remember...

* It's all right to argue and disagree It isn't the argument that counts. It's finding a solution, a compromise, or a way around the situation that you can both live with.
* Marriage is giving and taking. Love does mean having to say you're sorry.
* Nobody is perfect; we all make mistakes. Owning up to our mistakes is one of the most important things to learn and do.
* It's okay to go to bed angry. Sometimes, in order to say "I'm sorry" to someone else, you need time to realize that the words are true.
* Speak kindly to one another. Actions may speak louder than words, but words can cut right into someone's soul.

What do you need to work on in your marriage? We all have something that needs fixing. Ask the Holy Spirit for help in strengthening your love and commitment.

Lessons for Lasting Love January 20, 2016

Saint Valentine was a man who was willing to die to protect the right to marry. The couples he wed were willing to be imprisoned or killed for love. It would have been much easier for them to engage in sex or live together without bothering with marriage, but that's not what they wanted. They understood the importance of marriage, the sanctity of it, and the beauty of being husband and wife. It makes me sad that so many people today choose not to be married.

What would Saint Valentine think of our world and relationships today? Would he shake his head, perhaps even shed a tear, over modern views of marriage? If marriage was outlawed, or even just looked down upon, would he still risk his life or reputation to marry those who seek his help? Would we? Would couples even bother to marry? Would they risk their lives, their reputations, their self-reliance and pride, to take vows to have and to hold, from this day forward, for better, for worse, for richer, for poorer, in sickness and in health, to love and to cherish, till death do them part?

Do you value the sanctity of your vows? How can you make them work?

'Til Death Do Us Part February 13, 2019

Just before my father walked me down the aisle, he took me aside, held my hand. and said to me, "Amy, as a wife, and eventually a mother, it will be your responsibility to raise your family in the faith. You will need to make sure your husband goes to church and that your children are baptized and raised in our faith. It will be your most important job in life."

Of all the things my father could have said me at that moment, that's what he chose to say. It made such a profound impact on me that I still remember it and adhere to it all these years later.

Joseph never said a recorded word in the Bible, but his actions spoke volumes. He was a husband beyond reproach, a loving father who cared for and protected his son, a hard worker, a witness to his faith, and a "righteous man" who lived for others and for God.

My father is an example of a "righteous man." I hope that I have learned from his example and that I have raised my children to honor and respect their father as I do mine.

What example do you and your husband set for your children?

Go to Joseph, or to Dad   March 20, 2019

Mark Twain said, "No man or woman really knows what perfect love is until they have been married a quarter of a century."

My husband and I fall into that category, but sadly, so many today do not.

For those who are making their wedding plans or are still within that quarter of a century timeframe, always remember that the marriage is far more important than the wedding. Enjoy the time spent planning it, and know that it will not be perfect. Some small thing, or dare I say, maybe a big thing, will go wrong. Move on. It's a day, not a reflection of the rest of your life.

Face your marriage with love and humility. Take your vows seriously. Stand up before your friends and family in an actual church.

Treat your marriage like the sacred event that it is. Pray for your spouse and your marriage every day. Ask God to be a part of it, on that special day and always, for He is the rock upon which you can build a strong foundation.

Is God the foundation of your marriage?

Lessons for Lasting Love January 20, 2016

Don't let your wedding Mass be the only time you invite God into your relationship. He enters into it from the start and desires to stay with you always. Remember that "Those who trust in him will understand the truth, those who are faithful will live with him in love" (Wisdom 3:9).

God will never abandon you. Allow Him to be the rock upon which you build your marriage. When you build, make God the cornerstone. When you seek, allow Him to show you the way. When you wonder, be open to His wisdom. When you hurt, plead for His mercy. When you transgress, ask for His forgiveness. Do these together as a couple.

Pray together, fast together, go to Mass together, seek Him together. It truly is the only way your marriage will survive and prosper.

Finally, be a woman of worth, for "far beyond jewels is her value" (Proverbs 31:10).

May God bless your love and your marriage, lead you to prosperity and joy, and grant you a life filled with happily-ever-afters.

A Marriage of Worth May 15, 2019

*Q*ualities of True Leaders

"Remember your leaders, who spoke the word of God to you. Consider the outcome of their way of life and imitate their faith." - St. Paul to the Hebrews 13:7

Many people have favorite saints, people who set an example in life and intercede on our behalves when we need extra help. Many of these saints are seen by the world as flawless believers who never had a misstep or lapse of judgement, who never committed a sin or broke a law, and who never wavered in their faith in God and themselves. That assessment is very wrong. In fact, most of the saints made the same mistakes we make, but they didn't give up or give in. They worked every day to become the person that God knew they could be. The same goes for so many average individuals throughout history.

Successful people, like the saints, do not dwell on failure. They know that it's in seeing past the possibility of failure that we achieve success.

How are you working to be successful in the eyes of God?

"Without any doubting or quiddit"
September 21, 2016

We bow to athletes, politicians, and movie stars, hailing them as leaders and heroes. We tell our children, to be a leader is to be braggadocios, self-serving, rich, abusive, morally bankrupt, gluttonous, foul-mouthed, promiscuous, and lecherous. We teach that it's okay to lie, tear down, disparage, make fun of, and engage in debauchery. We forget that true heroes are ordinary people, going about their lives to the best of their ability.

Children need to learn about real heroes., people like Miriam, Ruth, Deborah, and Hannah. They should know the heroics of St. Peter and St. Paul and model themselves after Mother Teresa.

Let's stop hero-worship and promoting myths about greatness. Let's redefine leadership and heroism and recall the words of Isaiah, *"He who walks righteously and speaks uprightly, who despises the gain of oppressions, who shakes his hands, lest they hold a bribe, who stops his ears from hearing of bloodshed and shuts his eyes from looking on evil, he will dwell on the heights; his place of defense will be the fortresses of rocks; his bread will be given him; his water will be sure."*

Hero Worship and the Making of True Leaders
October 24, 2018

Strength is not about power.

As we are told in the Book of Psalms, "She [a woman of worth] is clothed with strength and dignity, and laughs at the days to come."

Clothed in strength, not exhibiting strength, not showing power or aggression or loftiness, but clothed in strength. That's quite remarkable when you think about it. Strength and dignity should be what we wear, what we exude, what we show others. It's more than being strong or powerful. It's letting others see what you're made of, but in a dignified way.

My mom is the matriarch of our family, and the bloodline that gives us life literally and figuratively, the glue that holds us together, giver of advice, and pillar on which we lean. Everyone thinks my father is the strong one, but, like the rest of us, his strength comes from Mom. It always has. She is my role model.

St. Paul told the Philippians, "I can do all things through him who strengthens me" (4:13).

Are you a model of strength to those around you? Who is your role model?

Five Things Mother Taught Me   May 10, 2017

When my father was fifty, he was diagnosed with cancer. He made a vow to Mary that, if she implored her Son to grant him just a few more years—enough time to see his children grow up–he would say a Rosary every day. My father is now in his eighties, and he says several Rosaries each day. He is a man of his word. He made a promise to Mary, and to God, and kept it.

How hard was it for Joseph to be a man of his word, to take Mary as his wife though she was pregnant? To sneak away in the night, with his wife and baby, leaving his family, friends, and job, in order to protect them? To teach his son all that he knew about God and scripture, all while knowing that his son was the son of God, the Messiah Himself?

Are you a person of your word, a witness to the faith, and a woman who lives her life for God and others?

Americans accept as fact the portrait of Washington crossing the Delaware, in which he looks confident, standing by the flag, the troops bravely battling the elements. But Washington could not have taken such a stance without tipping the boat, and the troops would not have had a clear, glowing sky leading them onward while the snow and wind raged on. More likely, Washington nervously held onto the wheel of the hastily constructed barge while the men, barely clothed for the cold, fought the weather and the current to make it safely across the river.

Why is this important? Because we often give leaders certain attributes they never possessed. We thrust greatness upon people, forgetting that they are just people. People are human. They make mistakes. They do things the wrong way. They have flaws and bad habits. They aren't always honest or moral. They aren't meant to be placed upon a pedestal, or to stand upright with their legs propped up on the side of a rowboat, lest they cause everything to be out of balance and go toppling into the waves.

Are you placing someone on a pedestal?

Hero Worship and the Making of True Leaders
October 24, 2018

Our parish held a women's retreat where we focused on the lessons of leadership in the lives of Miriam, Ruth, Deborah, and Hannah. These were women who sometimes made mistakes, who did not always do what society expected them to do, who had pasts that had to be overcome, who sinned and were redeemed.

However, all of these women strived for common goals: to be people of character, to hold fast to their faith, to counsel and advise, to teach others how to live virtuous lives, and to be women of God. They were not queens, not rulers, not rich, and not always revered. They had flaws, but they worked for the good of the people and taught others to do the same.

They weren't about power and glory (and when Miriam did become haughty, she was punished, served her time in exile, and was forgiven), but they were about doing what was right for the glory of God. Not themselves. For God.

What do you do for the glory of God?

Hero Worship and the Making of True Leaders
October 24, 2018

In Aladdin, the genie, a 'phenomenal cosmic power,' is the star. In Disney's animated version, Aladdin and the genie trick the evil sorcerer into wishing he was a more powerful genie, and he becomes trapped inside the lamp. The live-action version plays out almost the same BUT, Jafar does not wish to become the most powerful *genie* in the universe. In the retelling, he wishes to become the "most powerful *being* in the universe." The genie takes that to mean a more powerful genie, thus relegating Jafar to life in a lamp. All's well that ends well, but not with me.

The "most powerful *being* in the universe" is GOD. God is the source of miracles. God is the epicenter of all that is good, all that is possible, all that is known, and all that is unknown. He alone is the most powerful *Being* in the world. For Disney to change that one little word, is to change the universe. In a split second, Disney relegated God to being less than nothing when compared to the magic of a genie. But unlike the genie, God is real. He is the Alpha and the Omega. He is the real friend we all need.

Never let anyone or anything become more powerful than God in your life.

Phenomenal Cosmic Power May 29, 2019

*R*esting in the Lord

"Our hearts were made for You, O Lord, and they are restless until they rest in You."
- St. Augustine of Hippo

If you've taken a yoga class, you've heard the words, "If you need a break, come to child's pose." One morning, as we went into child's pose, on our knees with our heads bowed, those words really sank in for me. Typically, my mind goes to, *I don't need to go to child's pose. I don't need a break.* But when our instructor tells us to move on to downward dog, there's a voice in my head that says, *No, it feels good to be in child's pose!* That day, however, I had a revelation. We all need a break sometimes. We all need to come to child's pose.

Dropping to your knees isn't just for yoga. It's what we should do whenever we seek solace and rest. It's a meaningful moment, a plea for help or a break, a searching for peace of mind, for grace in your soul. When you need a break, come to child's pose.

"Let the little children come to me, and do not stop them; for it is to such as these that the kingdom of heaven belongs." Matthew 19:14

Come to Child's Pose December 16, 2015

I awake often at night. Sometimes, it's because Ken wakes, and since I can't sleep through the sound of a drop of rain on a blade of grass, I wake. Sometimes, it's the wind against the house, or a child using the bathroom, or Misty softly padding across the carpet. Whatever the noise, once I'm awake, there's no returning to sleep. I lie there for hours, hoping I can sleep. My body longs for slumber, but my mind refuses to shut down.

When I can't sleep, I pray. I pray rote prayers I learned as a child and long streams of consciousness that roll through the foggy recesses of my mind. There's never an end to my prayers—good health for my parents and Ken's mother, wisdom and happiness for my girls, success with a project, traveling mercies, intentions of friends and loved ones. I pray more at night when I'm trying to sleep than I do during the day when I'm fully awake.

Which makes me wonder...Maybe I'm doing it wrong when I'm awake. Maybe I'm supposed to be doing less and praying more. Maybe I need to spend less time focusing on me and more time focusing on God. It's not something I ever thought of before, but maybe it should have been.

Longing for a Little Sleep October 18, 2017

When I was a child, our family didn't have money to spare, but my brothers and I felt like we were the richest kids in the world. My parents took us to Andrews AFB to see the Blue Angels, to every Smithsonian Museum, up and down the hills at the National Zoo, laughing at the monkeys and marveling at the elephants. All of those things were free. To my parents, these were low-cost days spent with family. To my brothers and me, they were priceless days that made lasting memories.

Life can be overwhelming. We all need to take a break and do something fun now and then. Go outside. Connect with nature. Discover a passion. Enjoy time with your family. Play ball with your kids. Once, rather than taking a big, expensive vacation, we borrowed a friend's cabin in the Poconos. We hiked, zip lined, and even parasailed, but most of the trip was spent playing games, doing puzzles, and taking it easy. Morgan and her boyfriend, Jacob, spent hours fishing, and Ken and Katie enjoyed frequent naps. It was wonderful.

So, work when you must, but rest when you can. We all need a break sometime.

Withdraw From Your Cares May 30, 2018

We have no internet at our mountain cabin, limited cell service, and no house phone. The television, channels provided by satellite, is rarely on. Whether we are fishing in the lake at the bottom of the road, hiking the tall, round peak of Round Mountain that looms above our cabin, or sitting on the back deck, there is quiet and peacefulness that cannot be found in my normal world.

I love to spend a few minutes each day, basking in the glow of the sun that seems close enough to touch when standing at 10,000 feet above sea level. I close my eyes and enjoy that quiet peacefulness.

Our time in the wilderness is always over in the blink of an eye, and that peace and calm are feelings I want to remember, to take back with me when I return to civilization. The moment will have to last and sustain me until the next time we are able to carve out a few days, hopefully a couple of weeks, from our hectic routine to return to the mountains, to refresh our bodies and souls.

What is your favorite way to find peace and calm? Can you do that today?

Mountains, Body, and Soul July 11, 2018

Why do we appreciate a sunrise? Is it the beauty? God's promise of a new day? The knowledge that it will happen again tomorrow and the next day and the next? Maybe we long for that moment when all is peaceful. Maybe we're meant to marvel for a few minutes before the monotony of another day. We long for a bit of time when all is quiet, still and breathtaking?

We live in a world where everything moves quickly. Our days speed by in a flash of commotion, and we're left trying to catch our breath, wondering how it could be over so fast. We forget to look for that moment of peace.

If we stop, close our eyes, and allow the world to become quiet, we focus on where we are. We remember the pauses—those breathtaking moments. We spend each day working, running around, always trying to stay a step ahead, and we long for respite. "In vain you rise early and stay up late, toiling for food to eat—for he grants sleep to those he loves" (Psalms 127:2).

All the chaos, all the toiling, this race we find ourselves in, will come to an end. When we reach our Heavenly reward, we will finally be able to rest.

Savor the Moment. May 1, 2019

It was almost the end of our vacation when I awoke to discover spots covering my body. Ken rushed me to the nearest urgent care where I was diagnosed with Scarlett Fever—strep gone systemic.

The following week, I told my doctor that the spots would not go away. The doctor told me to spend 10 minutes every day outside in our pool.

Willing to do whatever it took, I dove into the pool. The water was warm and so soothing. I immersed myself in the luxurious liquid and then began swimming slow, easy laps. After a few minutes, I remembered how much I love to swim. I mean, I really, really love to swim. I began doing different strokes, racing back and forth from one side to the other. Then I just floated atop the water, letting it wash over me as I closed my eyes and relaxed in the glow of the late afternoon sun.

Whether it's an hour at the gym or a long, relaxing lunch, be sure to make a little bit of time for you. You deserve to prescribe some time each day to do something for yourself. If you slow down and take a few minutes for yourself each day, everyone around you will benefit, including you.

Prescription for Happiness. September 2, 2015

Setting the World on Fire

"Be who God meant you to be and you will set the world on fire!" - St. Catherine of Sienna

When I was young, I felt like the tree in the woods that wanted so desperately to be more than I thought I was—to have greener leaves, richer soil, more abundant birds nesting in my branches, and a greater amount of light shining on me. Though I think I hid it well, I was always insecure, never trusting that my friends were really my friends, always striving to be more than I felt I was, never sure that I was… enough.

Today, I know that I am who I am. I am enough. I am exactly who and what God intended me to be. I suppose I'm on my way to being like the oldest, tallest, and sturdiest trees in the forest.

You are enough. You are who God meant for you to be. Be happy with the person you are, use your God-given talents, and set the world on fire.

Seeing Through the Forest to the Trees
July 18, 2018

Everyone is born with a gift. The key is discovering what that gift is. Some people are born writers, others are born musicians, some are born actors. But those are truly only a small part of the world's population. Does that mean that only those in Hollywood, those on the New York Times bestseller list, or those filling stadiums to capacity every night are the only ones with talent? Of course not! I repeat, everyone is born with a gift.

Whatever it is that you do, do it well. Never lose sight of it. Pursue it with passion.

St. Paul tells us that "each man has his own gift from God, one in this manner, and another in that" (1 Corinthians 7:7).

We all have a talent. God wants us find the talent, be the best you can be at that talent, and show it to the world.

What is your talent? How can you show it to the world? Even better, how can you use it to glorify the one who gave it to you—God?

Be the Apple April 27, 2016

All of us have a need to feel fulfilled; and each of us is put here on Earth to serve a purpose. We each have our own meaning in life–the pursuit of that which makes us feel whole. For some, it's charity work. For others, it's a career. For others, it's providing a loving home for their families.

However, I find that what we think is our purpose in life is often what we've been told is our purpose—to have a good career, to make lots of money, to provide a big house with lots of stuff for our families.

The simple truth is, the life purpose of each person goes beyond what he earns or what she does for a living. It is that thing which makes us feel whole, that which inspires us to a higher calling.

What is your purpose in life? How are you being summoned to a higher calling?

Earning Fs in Life May 8, 2019

We should all strive to achieve great fortune in life–riches and wealth beyond compare.

However, these riches do not consist of the material things we own.

The wealth, of which I speak, is not the amount of money we have in the bank.

The fortune we should seek is that which encompasses our families, friends, faith, fun, and fulfillment.

We need to gather our family closer and cherish them. We need to collect good and faithful friends who will lift us up. We need to have the faith to move many mountains. We must amass hours of fun. We must search for what will lead us to fulfillment.

When we have all of those things, we all will have cups overflowing with the sweetest drink.

Count your blessings today. How wealthy are you? Can you even measure the fortune God has given you?

Earning Fs in Life May 8, 2019

*T*hese Three Remain: Faith, Hope, Love

"And now three remain: faith, hope and love. But the greatest of these is love" - *1 Corinthians 13:13*

My grandmother had a debilitating stroke and was going downhill fast; my father was diagnosed with cancer, again; one of our daughters was struggling with bullies; and we were in the process of trying to send all the girls to a private school. Ken unexpectedly resigned from his job; and just when I decided to stay home and get my writing career started, a tumor was discovered on my uterus that would require surgery and a biopsy. It seemed that my entire world was falling apart before my eyes, but this dark period in our lives taught me a very important lesson.

Have faith—always. I never let my faith waiver. I knew that God was going to provide. I knew trust God's will. I knew that whatever was to come, we could face it together. God came through in some very miraculous ways. Faith the size of a mustard seed can move mountains.

Lighting the Way This Christmas December 14, 2016

Rebecca's friends were spending the night, and the talk turned to weddings, as it often does with post-college girls! They told how their parents met, and each story was more charming than the last. Rebecca asked me to tell how Ken and I met. It's a lovely story that our family enjoys sharing, and it was obvious they all felt the same about their parents' first encounters.

They told of failed first marriages, high school sweethearts, second chance romances, and fate encounters. Each was different, but they all shared one quality— in the eyes of the girls, the stories were enchanting tales of falling in love and living happily ever after. Whether there was pain or strife involved, swirling snow or the perfect cup of cocoa, or a change meeting, the stories proved that the girls could all be featured in their own romance, just like their parents were.

All the girls made their parents' romances sound like Hallmark movies even if we all knew it was just an ordinary meeting between ordinary people destined for an ordinary life. Each story was special. The girls recognized that all of our stories have the potential to be a Hallmark story.

Make your Own Hallmark Story This Christmas
December 19, 2018

St. Paul tells us that "Love knows no limit to its endurance, no end to its trust, no fading of its hope; it can outlast anything. It is, in fact, the one thing that still stands when all else has fallen" (1 Corinthians 13: 7-8).

No truer words could be spoken about my mom. She loves her family fiercely and would do anything for them. The same can be said for her friends.

My love for my family and friends is a direct reflection of the love my mother has always shown to me and my brothers. It's a love without end, without restraints, without jealously. I think that the simplest way to describe the love that my mother gives is that it's a direct reflection of the Father's love for us.

Are you a direct reflection of the Father's love for us?

My dear friend, Alexandra Hamlet, once said, "Amy, you do not write romance novels. You write love stories."

All of my novels have a romance or two, but it's rarely the main thrust of the story. More often, there's an abundance of love going around that doesn't involve romantic love. My books are often about falling in love, but they really portray love of family, love of community, love of Country, and love of God.

With love, there is loss. There is hardship and pain, compromise and perseverance. Love is deeper than romance. It's more enigmatic than any mystery novel. It can generate faster heart-pounding than a suspense read. It's more mystical than a supernatural or paranormal tale. Love contains history, religion, and sometimes even elements of horror. Love is all-encompassing, and true love endures longer than the butterfly phase of even the greatest romance. Love is the one thing that can always make everything better.

As St. Teresa of Calcutta said, *"We can cure physical diseases with medicine but the only cure for loneliness, despair, and hopelessness is love."*

Telling Love Stories April 17, 2019

Like most characters learn by the end of a two-hour movie, your life, your story, your family's story, is what you make it. When we see our lives and the people in them as something special, unique, to be cherished, we can be just like the people on Hallmark. We may not have Balsam Hill trees or perfect sugar cookies in just fifteen minutes, but we do have the ability to see the wonder of life and to pass our stories along to our children.

At Christmas, if your family's rendition of *Silent Night* doesn't sound like a Blake Shelton-produced movie or your cookies aren't picture-perfect, don't worry. Your children will remember everything the way you make it out to be, whether it's *The Nightmare Before Christmas* or *It's a Wonderful Life.* You're living your own Hallmark movie every day. Write it the way you want it to be told, cherishing the good and bad, and smiling along the way. Celebrate the holidays with your own gingerbread house contest or a sleigh ride in the snow. Someday, you may look back and see your lives and your Christmases for what they really were—stories better than a Hallmark movie.

Make your Own Hallmark Story This Christmas
December 19, 2018

*U*nlock Your Self-esteem

"Before I formed you in the womb, I knew you." - Jeremiah 1:5

This world has very few *Davids*— Michelangelo's perfection in marble—but there are many *Slaves*—his imperfect, unfinished carvings.

As I was getting into the shower, I caught a glimpse of myself in the mirror. I looked at my inadequate body with its scars and rolls, far from the *David*. However, the scar that runs along my lower abdomen represents the three girls I brought into this world. The rolls I work so hard to get rid of are a result of carrying my children. The lines and shadows on my face trace the many joys and tears of a good life.

We're all slaves to our bodies, to the demands of society, to the inner voice saying us we aren't good enough, pretty enough, or sexy enough. It's time to break out of the marble that encases us and be slaves no more to the warped idea of perfection. It's okay to aim for perfection, but remember that humanity is far from perfect, unless of course, it's carved in stone.

Unbound   October 21, 2015

When I see friends with multiple children, I see true beauty, inside and out. When I look at someone who suffered from anorexia, I see a brave and strong person who can do anything she puts her mind to. When I see girls trying hard on the field or in the classroom, I see young women learning where and how they belong in this world. When I see scantily dressed girls, I wonder what they will do someday when faced with body fat, wrinkles, age spots. How will they adapt? Do they not know that their bodies will age, that there is much more they should be proud of?

Make a pledge today to become unbound. Stop complaining about the way you look. You are beautiful. If you don't like it, you can try to change it, but do it right. Let your daughters or those other young women in your life who look up to you see that you like yourself and that you're living a healthy lifestyle, looking out for your body's best interests but not trying to be something that society says you have to be. Do it not because you think someone else believes you should look a certain way. Point out the good in the women you know, not the flaws. We are not our bodies, and we are all beautiful in our own ways.

Unbound   October 21, 2015

I was ridiculed in high school for standing out, dressing my own way, being a little too loud and a little too peppy. I went through middle school feeling inferior to the popular girls, and I was determined not to do that in high school. No matter what, I was going to be myself.

There were girls who hated me and boys who were annoyed by me, but I didn't care. In the end, it didn't matter. I was never *in* the popular crowd, but I was friends with them, along with most other groups in school. I never tried to fit in with anyone, so I was able to fit in with everyone. And really, that's the way it should be. As everyone in my generation understands, "each one of us is a brain and an athlete and a basket case, a princess, and a criminal." It's when we stop hiding all of the facets of ourselves that we are able to show the real person beneath the mask.

There's an old adage that the least popular kids in high school are the most eligible ones twenty years down the line. So, be yourself. Don't worry about what others say or think, just be the best you that you can be. Take off your mask, and be proud of you. Life is too short to live in someone else's shoes, or their costume.

Unmasked October 28, 2015

Some of the most famous masterpieces of art—Botticelli's Birth of Venus, Michelangelo's David, Alexandros of Antioch's Venus de Milo—all have something in common; they all portray beautiful, naked depictions of the human body. They've been studied by art students for hundreds of years and recreated on posters, puzzles, signs, statues, and more. They're exquisite in detail and in beauty.

In America, the human body has been greatly devalued. The media portrays the body as little more than a sex item with nudity appearing only in pin-up magazines and pornography geared toward enticing sexual prowess. Women with 'perfect' bodies are glorified while any woman larger than a size 6 is chastised for her weight and size. Women are objectified rather than honored. We have lost all sight of what is beautiful and what is vulgar, and the result is that females in our society don't know whether to be comfortable with their bodies or ashamed of them.

We must teach our children to see the beauty in the bodies God gave them and to respect and honor everyone, regardless of how they look. We must start by seeing the beauty in ourselves.

Body Images July 29, 2017

I gazed at the sunset over the Sea of Galilee and watched the sun sink deeper toward the water. I thought about the reflection it cast and the reflection that I cast in my daily life. Each of us has two reflections. We all see the outer reflection that greets us when we stand in front of a mirror with our flaws exposed, but there is a reflection we cast which is only seen by the outside world. I wonder what I would see if I saw myself the way others do. If I were to gaze upon my own self, through another's eyes, would I see the person I see in my mirror, or someone I don't recognize at all?

The sun casts a reflection on the water, and what we see is the picture on the surface. But under the surface, the rays of the sun reach into the depths, the light creating beams and shadows, helping to create life and dispel darkness as far as they can extend. We need to be like the sun, showing a reflection that's more than skin deep, that reaches out to others, sustains life and hope, and dispels darkness and despair.

You and I will never walk on water like Christ did on the Sea of Galilee, but we can be a reflection of Him if we are willing to try.

Reflections February 3, 2016

I love Martha and Mary. In the story of Martha cooking and cleaning and Mary sitting at the feet of Jesus, Martha always gets the bad rap, but I would argue that the world needs both Marthas and Marys, and that we should all strive to be both.

The Marthas among us (regardless of the names) are doers. They are workers, inventors, crafters, movers and shakers. They teach, preach, and entertain. They stand up for what's right. They jump in and take over. They lead and command.

Marys are quiet, introspective, meditative, cautious, and prayerful. They remind us to slow down, smell the roses, and enjoy the little things in life. They are gentle, kind, and compassionate. They work quietly behind the scenes in places like classrooms, St. Vincent de Paul centers, churches, soup kitchens, and emergency services. They typically do as they are told, handmaidens beholden to one's word.

We all need to be Martha and Mary. We need to work, teach, preach, lead, and make things happen while taking time to be quiet, think, relax, enjoy, and pray. We need to know when we're called to act and when we're called to listen and reflect.

Are you a Mary or a Martha July 24, 2019

You spend your life wondering who you are, why you are here, what you are supposed to become. You ask why others don't understand you, and you worry that it is you, and it is, and that's okay because you are special.

Do not judge yourself by what others say or how others treat you. You have weathered it all and have come out on top and will continue to do so. You are a fighter, a healer, a lover, and friend. You are the best of everyone you know wrapped into one package.

Never forget that you alone will decide your course in life, but everyone around you will need your love and support to see them through, for you are a pillar standing tall, a beacon in the night, a refuge in the storm.

Most of all, you are strong, you are kind, you are love. The world is blessed because you are in it. You were created by God to be uniquely you. Embrace it.

Daughter, You Inspire Me January 6, 2016

$\mathcal{V}$alue every minute

"I always find a way of being happy."
- St. Therese of Lisieux

Make every occasion something to celebrate

I've said it before, but I'll say it again, life is short, and I firmly feel that we should take every opportunity to celebrate it.

It doesn't have to be an engraved invitation event. It can be a family dinner around that kitchen table. It can be a quiet walk on the beach. It can be a family game night or an afternoon boat ride. The type of celebration doesn't matter. What's important is taking the time to be together with family and/or friends and making everyone feel special.

Whether you're toasting a major milestone or just ticking off another year in the calendar of life, make those moments special. Your loved ones will remember that you cared enough to make something ordinary into something special, and it will inspire them to do the same.

What can you celebrate today?

Motherly Musings August 14, 2019

It's never enough to assume that others know how you feel. When Ken and I first began dating, over twenty-six years ago, I thought it was more than strange that his entire family says "I love you" every time they are on the phone. Without fail. It took me a long time to get used to hearing Ken tell his mother, father, brother, and sister that he loves them so often.

I'm not sure when the change began to occur in me. Perhaps it was when my father had his last bout with cancer. Maybe it was when Rebecca began driving or when my dear grandmother left us. At some point, I noticed that I, too, started saying "I love you" before saying goodbye.

Over the past two dozen years, we've lost grandparents, aunts, uncles, friends, and a dad. We've seen how quickly you can lose someone who meant more to you than you ever said out loud. The most important thing to remember is that it's not enough.

It's not enough to say I love you every now and then. It's not enough to wait until someone is dying to hold his hand, kiss his cheek, and whisper in his ear that you love him. It's simply not enough. Say it often, every day, every time.

It's Not Enough June 24, 2015

As the song asks, "how do you measure a year?" Three-hundred-and-sixty-five days. That's how we think of a year: a long, drawn out collection of days. But 365 is a small number that is gone in the blink of an eye. It sounds like a lot—five-hundred, twenty-five thousand, six hundred minutes. But in less than a year, a baby is conceived and then born, a wedding is planned, a school year is completed and another started, a fine wine ages, a house is built and occupied. And we look back and say, "where did the year go?" How does time get away from us so easily?

Think about all you did in the past year, the people you met, the places you visited, the things you accomplished. Think about the minutes that got away from you, the tasks left unfinished, the goals left unmet.

Don't think of the future as far away. Think of time as short and fleeting. Make the most of every day, every minute. There's much to be seen in the world, many new people to meet, and a lot to be accomplished.

The reality is, there is never enough time in which to do it all, but there is enough time to enjoy life. How can you start today?

How Do You Measure A Year? December 7, 2016

I feel like I'm chasing a thief, trying to lure it into a trap. Where is he hiding my precious moments? How do I get them back? I blink, and time has passed. I close my eyes, and the year is coming to a close. I turn, and my girls are grown and gone.

Those stolen moments make me I realize I am the one caught in a trap. I'm the one who allows the thief to enter, emboldened by my own willingness to let him take those minutes, those hours, those days in return for a few seconds of happiness. I am the one who turned my life into a race along the shore, where the water weighs down my feet as I try to make progress while the waves mock my futile steps.

I must find a way to work with the thief of time. I will make room in my calendar for the minutes that matter. I will accept the crises and the glitches, as well as the unexpected pleasures, and make them work together to slow the sand in the hourglass. For one day, the thief will take the last granule of sand, and I will be left to wonder if I used the grains to build castles with open drawbridges or walls and moats. Time, like all gems, is rare, precious, and to be handled with care.

Slipping Sand into Precious Pearls
November 14, 2018

The older I get, the more I realize that everything slips from our grasp too quickly, and I am led to wonder how I make it stop. How can I slow down time? How can I make sure I don't miss a thing? I once read a thought by Bishop Robert Barron, "An image that always comes to mind when I think of these things is the gorgeous firework that bursts open like a giant flower and then, in the twinkling of an eye, is gone forever. Everything is haunted by nonbeing." This is not a bad thing, this reminder that all things fall into nonbeing. It can be a wonderful thing.

There is a blessing to be found in the nonbeing. What is it and how do we find it?

We can take a pause in the morning or evening to marvel at the sunrise or the sunset. We can ooh and ah at a fireworks display. We can hold that newborn, kiss her sweet-smelling forehead, and take in the scent of her newness. We can celebrate every milestone: every anniversary, birthday, graduation, new job, or new adventure. We can remind ourselves every day that we are to look for those precious moments and savor them.

Savor the Moment May 1, 2019

Wonderful Adventures: Seeking God

"Life with Christ is a wonderful adventure."
St. John Paul the Great

I believe there are many out there in need of something, and they have no clue what that something is.

Over and over, I've heard people say that they didn't know they needed God until they found Him. He is there, waiting to be found, and He is a friend who never fails, never falters, never turns His back on those who love Him.

God is a shelter, a treasure, an elixir of life. Once you have found Him, you will realize that it was Him that you needed all along.

I Didn't Know I Needed You... April 25, 2018

1 Kings 19, 11-13 is one of the most beautiful scripture passages, and I marvel at how the story of Elijah is repeated every day in our own lives.

Then the LORD said: Go out and stand on the mountain before the LORD; the LORD will pass by. There was a strong and violent wind rending the mountains and crushing rocks before the LORD—but the LORD was not in the wind; after the wind, an earthquake—but the LORD was not in the earthquake; after the earthquake, fire—but the LORD was not in the fire; after the fire, a light silent sound. When he heard this, Elijah hid his face in his cloak and went out and stood at the entrance of the cave.

In the grandeur and glory of life, the frantic pace to be in front of the crowd, the bright lights and festive music, and in the myriad of decorations and parties and feasts, Jesus comes to us in the simplest form.

He comes in a little bit of prayer time in the midst of a hectic day. He comes among the messiness of the stable and the crying of the animals, the messiness of life and the noise around us. He is waiting for us to come to Him and to listen for Him in the silence. Will you listen for Him today?

Listening to the Silence December 12, 2018

In the television show, *Friended By God*, Miles decides he no longer wants to hear from God, and he does what so many others do in the real world. He unfriends God. By the end of the show, he is remorseful, so he goes to Facebook and re-friends God.

immediately, God accepts.

How often have we had to do re-friend God? How often do we have days, weeks, months, years, when we abandon our friendship with God?

The beautiful thing is that God always accepts us back as a friend—immediately. There is no time too long and no distance too far, for a new or renewed friendship with God. He is waiting for you.

"I will give them a heart to know me, that I am the LORD. They shall be my people and I will be their God, for they shall return to me with their whole heart." - Jeremiah 24:7

Will you accept?

Sometimes we spend hours, days, or years searching for something we believe is 'out there,' just beyond our grasp, often right in front of us but hidden from view. Many people turn to alcohol or drugs, thinking those will lead them to answers, but it hinders their search. They hide rather than seek truth. Some people cling to unhealthy relationships, looking for someone to show them their purpose instead of seeking wisdom and answers from God. Some ignore truth altogether, searching for wants instead of needs.

Think about The Prodigal Son. Talk about searching! The young man was on a search for happiness, fulfillment, perhaps his purpose in life. Maybe he didn't know what he was even searching for. He believed whatever he was seeking could not be found in his father's house, so he left in search of answers. He searched in far-off lands, in dens of darkness and sin, and "squandered his inheritance on a life of dissipation" (Luke 15:13). When he didn't find what he was searching for, he returned home where his father waited with open arms. God waits for us with open arms. He has known you and loved you for all eternity. Seek Him out today.

Searching for Answers April 3, 2019

I spend a lot of time while traveling visiting churches and monasteries. Why? Because in so many countries, that's where all the history is, and it's where God is. While in Bruges, Belgium, Rebecca and I found ourselves among a small group of people visiting a local church. Well, unbeknownst to us, one of Michelangelo's *Madonnas* stood in a corner of the church, and we got to see it. A year or so later, I sat in a dark movie theater and watched George Clooney and company save the *Bruges Madonna* from the Germans. Until *The Monuments Men* came out, I'm guessing most tourists would not have thought to visit that beautiful church, one of the highlights of our stay in Bruges.

One of highlights of a trip to Corinth, Greece, was walking among the ruins where St Paul preached.

No matter where you're going or what you're doing, pray that the Holy Spirit can be your guide. Let God lead you or seek Him out. Send a message to your children, reminding them that God is in all places and all things, and that it's important to seek Him out and make Him part of your life, even on vacation. God is always there, waiting to be found.

A Mother/Daughter Adventure June 12, 2019

e𝒳pect God to Be There For You

"Because grace and mercy are upon his elect, and he watches over his holy ones." - Wisdom 3:9

When I was a little girl, I attended my first musical, *Annie*, and spent the following weeks memorizing every word to every song. I've never stopped singing those songs and enjoyed watching Rebecca and then Katie play roles in school and community productions of the same play. As a child, I'm not sure I realized how many lessons I was learning from the little orphan girl who took in a stray dog and softened the heart of a grouchy, old millionaire, but I have always remembered and adhered to her words "the sun will come out tomorrow."

Things change, people are lost, the world is shaken, but the sun still rises, and human beings continue living, striving for the best, reaching for the stars, and living the good life as best they can.

And every night, we go to bed with the knowledge that no matter what happens in the world, the sun will come up tomorrow and that God is still there no matter what.

Just Thinking About Tomorrow November 25, 2015

Ken and I were newly married and in a tight spot. We were more than stretched thin—two young kids in their twenties who spent every cent they had on a house. I was working on my master's. Ken was working three jobs and applying for loans to attend law school.

One Sunday, we quarreled on our way to Mass. I was writing a check for the weekly offering, and Ken said we didn't have the money to spare. I felt we had enough to give a small portion to the church. After a short debate, he grudgingly relented. We put our check in the basket and moved on.

Two days later, Ken realized he had forgotten to pay the mortgage. It was due the next day, and we had nothing left in our bank account. Guilt consumed me.

I did the only thing I could. I prayed. The next day, Ken was getting ready for job number two when he stopped. Reaching onto a high shelf, he picked up a tin and shook it. He opened it and pulled out a wad of cash he'd forgotten about. It was the exact amount of our mortgage payment.

I was relieved but not surprised. Jesus told us in Luke 6:38, "Give, and it will be given to you." It's a lesson we will never forget.

Giving More March 1, 2017

I'm not a worrier, never have been. I keep my chin up and my spirits bright. God carries my worries, and my burden is light. However, I'm always keeping my eye to the sky, recognizing that having faith is not the same as being oblivious to the storm.

Once, I sat in my car outside at the pool, waiting to hear if Morgan's swim meet was cancelled. I was shocked when I saw Morgan climb onto the block and dive into the pool as the wind whipped through my open windows and the clouds darkened to an ominous, charcoal color. Were they actually letting the kids go into the water? Was nobody going to acknowledge the coming storm? Why weren't they cancelling the meet? I watched the clouds roll in, and raindrops began to ping on my windshield, growing more intense each second. Within minutes, the sky cleared, and the meet went on as planned.

While I still believe that we need prepare and watch for the coming storms, I was reminded that night that it's sometimes even more important to just have faith that all will turn out the way it was meant to be. Carry your umbrella, but have faith that the clouds will part, and trust that the storms will lead to a sunnier future.

Seeking the Silver Lining August 3, 2016

Free your mind from worries. Don't fret over problems, large or small, that are out of your control. Don't become anxious over things that you cannot change. Remember that you cannot control all things and all people. You can only control how you react to them. React with patience, with kindness, and with love. Seek peace from your faith, and know that God has a plan for you. Put your trust in Him, forsaking all worries, and know that He will lead you down the path for which you were chosen. When in doubt, pray.

When times of worry strike, when anxiety overtakes you, find solace in the things that bring you joy. Take a break and visit someone who always makes you feel good. Spend just a few minutes with the Lord. Treat yourself to something that makes you happy. Reflect on all the good times you've had. Turn to someone who makes you smile. There are many times in life when a smile is all that is needed to cure whatever ails you.

Know that God is there, waiting for you to ask for help. He is always just a prayer away.

Dear Graduate, Be Happy May 22, 2019

*Y*ielding to God's Will

"To walk out of his will is to walk into nowhere." - C.S. Lewis

We live in a culture of death. We hear stories every day about assisted suicide and compassionate death, about the most vulnerable among us having no say in whether they live or die, about families being encouraged to "pull the plug."

These were our thoughts as Ken and I drove home from the theater. We believe it was all part of God's perfect plan that the boy in *Breakthrough* was sent to Cardinal Glennon, a Catholic hospital. We believe that John's story may be a message to the world, a plea from God: "Do not be conformed to this world but be transformed by the renewal of your mind, that you may prove what is the will of God" (Romans 12:2). We believe that John's story and others like it are reminders that life is sacred. God is the divine physician Too many have bought into the lie that extinguishing life is the greater good.

May we always have the courage and strength to let God be God and man be man.

A Breakthrough in Life April 24, 2019

The 40th Psalm tells us, "To do your will, O my God, is my delight." In the midst of all the chaos that surrounds me, I am reminded that I can't always be in control. I should bow joyously to God's will. Sometimes, I have to let things happen slowly, to let situations come about of their own accord, to deal with the dust and the dirt and the noise of this everyday life without trying to make things happen in my own time and in my own way. I have to remind myself to delight in what God has in store. It's so hard!

Patience is a virtue. We hear it so often that we forget that there is truth in the saying. I know I do! Perhaps God enjoys throwing us curveballs, blocking our path, or forcing us to endure long, drawn-out trials, both large and small, in order to remind us that we are just one small presence in this world. We are to live our lives for Him and for others, finding patience when we are being tested and acceptance when we can't be in control. Until then, we need to bear all things and be satisfied with each small step, looking forward to what is to come. God is in control in all ways and in all things. I need to remind myself, when my stress level rises, that He has this.

Patience is a Virtue I am Lacking October 25, 2017

One of my favorite sayings is, we plan, God laughs.

I don't believe in coincidence but in the perfection of God's plans. Everything happens according to His plan, not ours.

Like young Mary and the carpenter, Joseph, we make plans. We lay out what we want our lives to be like. We make lists, keep calendars, set times. And then God steps in.

Mary understood this. Years after accepting God's plan for her life, in the town of Cana, she told the wine stewards, "Do whatever He tells you." And to her son, she merely let it be known that God decides when one's time has come. So, what did the stewards and the son of Mary do? They said, "yes" to Mary and to God.

Here's what I know: when God calls to me, when He invites me to join Him, when he asks me to alter my plans and trust Him, I will remind myself that, no matter what my own plans may be, God expects me to give a very loud, firm, and resounding, YES.

Are you ready to say, Yes, to God?

Emphatically, Yes February 6, 2019

Zealous Parenting

"As the family goes, so goes the nation, and so goes the whole world in which we live."
St. John Paul the Great

George Lucas said that Steven Spielberg once told him, he hopes to die on a movie set. Lucas said he hopes to die in bed watching a Spielberg movie.

When asked, "And how do you want to be remembered?" Lucas gave the simplest yet most profound answer, "As a good dad."

After the life he has lived, a man who will be immortalized through the stories he created wants to be remembered simply as "a good dad."

Is it any wonder that in his greatest story, it was because of the love for his child that the father sacrificed everything he had, everything he worked toward, even his own life to save his son?

In the end, it was not his actions as a villain that most people recount when speaking of Vader, but as a father. Lucas knew all along that fame, fortune, and power are trivial, and that being a parent is what truly matters.

"I am your father..." December 30, 2015

When Katie told me I'm her best friend, I knew she didn't mean I was a party buddy or someone who would condone every bad move she makes. She meant that I was the one she could count on to be there for her, good and bad, and tell her like it is, whether she wants to hear it or not.

When Morgan's friends marvel that she has no secrets from me, she understands that having no secrets also means I get to reprimand her when she is wrong and punish her when she does something of which I don't approve.

When Rebecca was recuperating after oral surgery, she knew I was going to make her follow the doctor's orders because that's what moms do. She also knew, no matter how tired I was, I would stay up to watch another movie with her.

I will never feel bad for being friends with my girls. They know when I am Mom and when I am their friend. As with my mother, there are lines that are not crossed. But they also know that I will be there for them, the only true best friend they will ever have, from the day they were born through all eternity.

Why It's OKAY To Be Friends With Your Kids
March 2, 2016

It's not easy telling my children no. I always want to say yes. I want to give them everything their hearts desire. I want to hand them the moon and sprinkle it with stars. I want to make all of their dreams come true and let them do whatever they want to do and go wherever they want to go. But I can't, and there's a very good reason why.

I can't because I love them.

I tell them, do not ask me again why I said no. Do not question why I'm not the mom who shrugs and says yes to everything.

I know they still won't understand. It will take years for them to comprehend why I am being so mean, not letting them spread your wings, and not letting them make their own decisions and their own rules. I know they will be angry. I know they will say, "everyone is doing it," or "you can trust me." I also know that way of thinking can lead to disastrous consequences.

And I know that someday, they will thank me.

Someday, You'll Understand July 20, 2019

Raising our girls hasn't always been easy, and it hasn't always been fun, but it has been worth all of the effort, all of the tears, and all of the pain because there has been so much fun, laughter, and joy. However,…

I wish I read to my girls later. One day, I turned around I realized it had been years since I had cuddled in bed with one of my girls and read to or with her. It ended way too soon, and I regret not finding ways to stretch it out.

I wish I had played with them more.

I wish I had told them they don't have to always be on the top of the heap. I should have told them to try their best, work their hardest, and reach for the stars but not at the expense of their self-worth, sanity or integrity. I wish I had told them it's okay to fail as long as you try again.

I wish I had paid more attention to my girls when they talked. I'm always distracted, always thinking about what I should be doing, always trying to complete several tasks at once.

I hope they know that I tried, I sometimes failed, but I always loved them whether I remembered to tell them that or not.

Seven Things I Should Have Done August 29, 2018

I wish I had shown my girls the real world.

We traveled a lot, and they saw amazing sights and had unforgettable experiences in places all over the world. But we never served at a soup kitchen. We never visited a homeless shelter. We took many loads of clothes and goods to St. Vincent de Paul, but we didn't give enough of our time as volunteers.

When Rebecca was a Junior Girl Scout, she earned her Bronze Award by collecting back packs and school supplies and handing them out to underprivileged children through St. Vincent de Paul. She still talks about the little boy who cried as he hugged his backpack as if it was a bag full of gold and precious jewels.

Morgan talks about the man with the broken bike which she and another volunteer helped fix. When the man left, Morgan learned that he was homeless, and the bike was his only possession. But we never did anything with that knowledge. We never even tried.

I wish we had made sure that the girls did more to help others. What can you do with your kids to help others?

Tell your children what you expect of them instead of what you hope they will do.

* I expect you to be a leader and not follow others down the wrong path.

* I expect you to follow our rules and the law and not drink, smoke, or do drugs.

* I expect you to abstain from sex because you're not ready, you're not married, and you're not equipped to handle the consequences.

* I expect you to study hard and get good grades.

There's a big difference between telling a child, "this is what I expect you to do and how I expect you to behave" and saying, "you shouldn't do this, but if you do, do it safely." That's certainly part of the conversation but shouldn't be the focus.

The focus should be creating expectations and teaching them that it's not only okay to stand their ground, but it will be better for them in the long run.

Raising children is a lot like raising puppies. You discipline as best you can, hoping they understand that it's out of love.

You scold and yell to stop them from doing something harmful

You keep them on a short leash for as long as you can; but then you realize that there comes a day when you have to trust them, leave them alone, let them wander, and pray that when you or they return, nothing has been damaged beyond repair.

There will be accidents and incidents, and no matter how old they are, they will try your patience and make you so angry you see red, but deep down, you know that all they really want from you is your love and attention.

Loving them while letting them go is the hardest thing I've ever done, but I know that someday we will all reap the rewards.

Raise your children with love, a healthy dose of fear, and with an abundance of faith and trust in God.

Raising Adults October 14, 2015

*A*bout the Author

Amy began writing as a child and never stopped. She wrote articles for magazines and newspapers before writing children's books and adult fiction. A graduate of the University of Maryland with a Master of Library and Information Science, Amy worked as a librarian for fifteen years and, in 2010, began writing full time.

Amy writes inspirational women's fiction for people of all ages. She has published two children's books and numerous novels, including the award-winning Picture Me, Whispering Vines, and the Chincoteague Island Trilogy. A former librarian, Amy enjoys a busy life on the Eastern Shore of Maryland.

The recipient of numerous national literary awards, including the Illumination Award, LYRA award, Independent Publisher Book Award, International Digital Award, and the Golden Quill Award as well as honors from the Catholic Press Association, the Eric Hoffer Book Award, and the American Book Fest Award, Amy's writing has been hailed "a verbal masterpiece of art" (author Alexa Jacobs) and "Everything you want in a book" (Amazon reviewer). Amy's books are available internationally, wherever books are sold, in print and eBook formats.

Follow Amy at:

http://amyschislerauthor.com

http://facebook.com/amyschislerauthor

https://twitter.com/AmySchislerAuth

https://www.goodreads.com/amyschisler

Also by Amy Schisler

Novels

A Place to Call Home

Picture Me

Whispering Vines

Summer's Squall

The Devil's Fortune

Chincoteague Island Trilogy

Island of Miracles

Island of Promise

Island of Hope

Children's Books

Crabbing With Granddad

The Greatest Gift

Collaborations

Stations of the Cross Meditations for Moms

(with Anne Kennedy, Susan Anthony,

Chandi Owen, and Wendy Clark)